Satanism

Ted Schwarz & Duane Empey

Is Your Family Safe?

Satanism

Zondervan Books
Zondervan Publishing House
Grand Rapids, Michigan

SATANISM

Copyright © 1988 by Ted Schwarz and Duane Empey

Zondervan Books are published by Zondervan Publishing House,
1415 Lake Drive, S.E., Grand Rapids, Michigan 49506

Library of Congress Cataloging in Publication Data

Schwarz, Ted, 1945–
   Satanism / Ted Schwarz & Duane Empey.
   p. cm.
ISBN 0-310-45041-1
   1. Satanism. I. Empey, Duane. II. Title.
BF1548.S38   1988
133.4′22—dc19

88-21620
CIP

In several chapters, names have been changed. In some instances,
people requested it. In others, it was done to avoid harassment or
retribution. In a few instances, such as the story of the Cambridge
family, a number of criminal activities are mentioned for which no
charges have been brought. Although extensive documentation is
available concerning ritual child abuse, drug abuse, and murder,
charges have not been filed due to technicalities relating to the
statute of limitations, the unwillingness of witnesses to testify, and
similar difficulties; so names again were changed. These changes
have been infrequent throughout the text of this book, but it is
important for the sake of accuracy to note these.

Printed in the United States of America

88 89 90 91 92 93 / PP / 10 9 8 7 6 5 4 3 2

CONTENTS

DEVILBOOK: AN INTRODUCTION 7

DEVIL THEORY

1. DEVILDOM WEST: CALIFORNIA STYLE 13
2. DEVIL LORE: FRENCH FIRST BUT NOT LAST 27

DEVILS ON HORSEBACK

3. DEVIL-BRIDE: HEATHER CAMBRIDGE 41
4. DEVIL-TONGUE: TED RABOUIN 57
5. DEVIL-DANCER: ANTON LAVEY 69
6. DEVIL-ADVOCATE: MICHAEL AQUINO 95

DEVILRY

7. DEVIL-GAMES: DUNGEONS & DRAGONS? 121
8. DEVIL-SONGS: ROCK & ROLL? 141

DEVIL-MARKS

9. DEVIL-GIRL: JESSIE? 165
10. DEVIL-CHILDREN: UNTOLD ABUSE! 177

DEVIL-DODGING: FINAL THOUGHTS 192

DEVILBOOK:
AN INTRODUCTION

He is Satan, the Devil, the Evil One, the Adversary. To some, he is the justification for minor human failings, thus, the phrases "The Devil made me do it" and "full of the Devil."

To others, he is the key to power, fame, and fortune. He is the charismatic leader of the self-confessed losers who have decided that God has failed them. Their lives are without meaning, so they turn to what they perceive to be the only source of pleasure.

To yet others, he offers an intellectual challenge. In God, we are restricted and unable to choose a more pleasurable way. Satan worship, especially in its more intellectual forms, provides a chance to unlock the secrets of the universe, to step outside the mundane, the ordinary, the structured, into a world only a privileged few ever attain.

Historically, Satan has most specifically been defined within the New Testament. The name represents that evil power who stands in opposition to God but is always subject to God's will. The Lord's Prayer and the parable of the sower speak of the Evil One (Matt. 6:13; 13:19). The Devil tempts Christ and is later called "a liar and the father of lies" (Matt. 4:1; John 8:44).

The concept for John Milton's *Paradise Lost* probably came from Isaiah 14:12–15, which speaks of one who has "fallen

7

from heaven." Yet the concept of Satan as an evil power seems not to have taken full root until such New Testament passages as Mark 3:22–30, which speaks specifically of Satan as a prince of demons ruling an underworld of evil.

Satan stands at odds with God's purpose for mankind and can have great influence over the affairs of man, but in the end he is always subject to limitations. The teaching most children receive, that good is always greater than evil, has a biblical basis. No matter how insidious the work of Satan, he is never a match for God.

In recent times, Satan, like the Bible, seems to have become a scapegoat for the bigots, the crazies, the troubled, and the lost. Many otherwise well-educated individuals define whatever they fail to understand as satanic, a term that may mean anything from the way their son has his hair cut to the fact that the minister of their church developed hemorrhoids. Some believe that good people receive financial rewards and evil people invite suffering. A "good Christian" is a wealthy man or woman, blessed with the Mercedes-Benz and the expensive suburban home. Those who have "fallen away" to Satan are likely to live in a regular apartment because condominiums, by this line of thinking, are the first outward and visible signs of God's grace. They drive a secondhand Chevrolet or, worse, are forced to take the bus.

Other misguided people say that there is no Satan because a loving God is incapable of allowing evil to dominate eternity. There is no Satan; there is no hell; and evil is only the freewill choice of man from which he will eventually be saved.

This book is not a ponderous theological treatise on the nature of good and evil. It is not an attempt to show how Satan is walking among us in the last days before Armageddon. Instead, it is an overview of contemporary Satanism and the people who have chosen to worship the Adversary.

The book reveals the reality of Satan worship today. Although some Satanists dress in black robes and have inverted crucifixes, altars for naked women, and stolen wafers from Catholic mass in their homes, most are likely to be similar to your friends and neighbors. The contemporary Satanist is more likely to be the kindly doctor who cared for your aged parent during the final stages of a painful terminal illness than the dirty, long-haired, wild-eyed drifter with "Born to Kill" tattooed on his arm. The lawyer who gives you advice, the dedicated social worker, the college professor, the auto mechanic who works on your car, these are the people whose private lives too frequently hold secrets both perverse and shocking. The leader of the Temple of Set, a group that broke away from the Church of Satan, is a lieutenant colonel in the U.S. military, a holder of a top secret clearance, a linguist, and a Ph.D. in political science who has worked with NATO. Others have been police officers, staff doctors in major hospitals, and seemingly loving, gentle housewives and mothers who work part or full time at day-care centers.

The number of people who practice Satan worship in its various forms is not large. Yet the individuals and groups who have chosen to seek the powers they believe can only come from Satan are numerous enough that they are likely to form *that other church down your block.*

DEVIL THEORY

DEVILDOM WEST: CALIFORNIA STYLE

The story could begin at any time in history. Satan worship, in one form or another, is as ancient as human existence and as contemporary as today's headlines. We are beginning the story in the 1950s because that era was similar to today and the time when contemporary Satanism first came to America.

FEARFUL FIFTIES

For many Americans, the memory of the 1950s has been distorted through epithets like the Silent Generation and television shows such as "Happy Days" and "Laverne and Shirley." For religious leaders with short memories, it was a golden age for the American church. Family worship was at an all-time high, and numerous magazines devoted articles to such subjects as "Why I am proud to be a Baptist" or "Why I am proud to be an Episcopalian."

The 1950s also were extremely unpleasant. America was permeated with fear—of the communists, of the atomic bomb, of spies, and even of violating the strict conformity in the business world. This was the era of the "cold war," a time when many believed there would be an ultimate struggle for world domination at any moment. It was also a time when the American way of life was synonymous with intense consumerism, conformity, and the belief that a person's worth was determined by the location of one's home, the type and newness of the car one drove, and the type of job one held.

The 1950s produced the first generation of American children raised with the fear of early death. At any moment Russia's atomic bombs might come raining down upon their heads. President Harry Truman began a nationwide civil defense program with the words, "I cannot tell you when or where the attack will come or that it will come at all. I can only remind you that we must be ready when it does come."

As if to emphasize his point, Operation Wakeup was staged in Los Angeles in 1951. A plane dropped two million leaflets over the city, alerting each reader that he or she would now be a casualty if the falling leaflets had really been Russian atomic bombs.

Atomic bomb drills were held in schools across the nation. Every child learned how to "duck and cover" when the air raid sirens were sounded. "Duck and cover. That's the way. We can beat those Russkies any day." Under your desk, face to the floor, eyes closed, arms over your head, then wait for the "all clear" to sound.

There were also drills for home use. "Stay away from windows. Try to go near a solid wall. If one isn't available, go under a heavy table or huddle under a mattress. Then duck and cover and wait for the all clear."

Television shows had public service spots to show children how to survive in the outdoors. A little boy was happily pedaling his bicycle in one such commercial. He heard the air raid siren, leaped from his bike, raced to a convenient ditch by the side of the road, then ducked and covered. It was a simple trick that assured American survival. The war would come;

the bombs would explode; but, in the end, Russia was certain to lose. Their people weren't prepared. They didn't know how to duck and cover.

The paranoia spread to the construction industry. Bomb shelters became as much a part of the American landscape as tract homes. Deluxe models ran $3,000 and would enable a family of five to survive for up to five days. Less expensive but better publicized was the $1,995 model of Mrs. Ruth Colhoun, who began her shelter construction amid typical Hollywood fanfare in January of 1951. As television cameras rolled and Hollywood starlets looked on, Mrs. Colhoun explained to reporters, "It will make a wonderful place for the children to play in and it will be a good storehouse, too. I do a lot of canning and bottling in the summer, you know." Going to the bomb shelter would be a little like having a picnic in the park. After three or four days underground, it would be safe to get on with our lives, secure in the knowledge that the Russians had been annihilated because they didn't have the foresight to build their own shelters before the bombs hit.

Some debated moral issues such as whether or not to shoot your best friend if, shelterless, he tried to get into your shelter. Usually such issues were never resolved, though wealthier individuals built shelters large enough for their friends. Mrs. Alf Heiberg, previously married to General Douglas MacArthur, designed a shelter large enough to hold one hundred people. And Colonel Robert McCormick, publisher of the *Chicago Tribune,* constructed a shelter to hold his entire staff.

Despite the optimistic attitude expressed by such plans, impending death and ultimate destruction still were all pervading. These fears were furthered by the events of the day. During a speech on January 31, 1950, Truman authorized the Atomic Energy Commission to move steadily into the construction of new super bombs. The next month, Albert Einstein, internationally renowned scientist, declared that mankind now held the capability to destroy the earth through radiation poisoning of the atmosphere. And by June, North

Korea invaded the Republic of South Korea, proof that communism was on the march. Three years later, with war still raging in Korea, the Soviet Union's premier, Georgi Malenkov, announced that Russia possessed the hydrogen bomb.

For teenagers of the day, it was obvious that there might be no future, no hope of having the pleasures of the adult world. Their lives would be aborted in an orgy of violent death no matter how often they practiced responding to the call of "duck and cover."

To add to the fears and frustrations, the 1950s was a period of extreme class consciousness, a time when you became what you purchased. The prewar generation had avoided spending money. You worked, you saved, and you purchased for cash whatever you desired.

World War II saw millions of Americans working in defense plants, earning large sums of money and having nowhere to spend it. By the 1950s, Madison Avenue had discovered the power of television to entice the public to buy. Advertising implied that a man was what he owned, and stores cooperated by stressing credit accounts, "charge-a-plates," and layaway plans. By 1957, Cadillac offered the El Dorado Brougham with such basic necessities as lipsticks, perfume bottle, tissue dispenser in the dashboard, a vanity case, and four gold-finished drinking cups. General Motors shunned safety and proudly announced that they had improved the sound of their slamming door. They convinced the public that such a sound would tell the world that they owned a big car.

Tract housing was invented on a grand scale by William J. Levitt, who introduced Levittowns of mass produced, identical, boxlike houses in Long Island, New York, and just outside Philadelphia. Each house had trees planted every twenty-eight feet (two and one-half trees per home) and came equipped with an Admiral television and a Bendix washer, refrigerator, and stove. The tracts were so uniform that there were rules related to the types of devices that could be used for drying clothing and which days of the week would be "proper" for their use. Everyone was expected to conform, but advertisers appealed to an individual's status consciousness by implying that even in a tract home, one could become someone special by buying a power lawn mower, installing a second bathroom, adding air conditioning, or even goldplating the existing bathroom fixtures.

The good life was constantly being threatened, however. Not only the bomb, of course, but also the deadly red menace spawned fear. Senator Joseph McCarthy inflamed America by finding communists in every government agency, only a handful of whom he ever was able to name. In Michigan, beatings of automakers were common. All a man had to do was refuse to express outright hatred of the communist menace, and he would find himself bloodied, often in plain sight of uniformed police officers who sided with the attackers. Best-selling books and movies evolved from the pens of former FBI agents and men who had secretly joined communist groups in order to serve as spies and informants.

Anyone who spoke in favor of social change, no matter how necessary, was likely to be vilified as un-American. People ignored the primitive sanitation and inhuman working condition in migrant farm labor camps for fear of being called agitators. Racial segregation, urban poverty, and similar social concerns were seldom mentioned by newspapers and magazines. Such reality was too dangerous for those who might dare to call attention to it.

The family was considered to be the future of America in the 1950s. The father was king of the household, and everything had to be planned around his needs. Parents and society encouraged women to avoid both advanced education and a career because their place was in the home, raising the children, meeting the husband's physical and sexual needs, and sympathizing when he had to go out "with the boys" for intellectual stimulation. Women were mentally and physically inferior, creatures to be sheltered and enjoyed but seldom

17

respected. The most liberated woman on television was Lucy of "I Love Lucy" in which the brilliant comedienne Lucille Ball played an addlepated clown whose continuing disasters were lovingly tolerated by her husband.

The role man played was all important, whether he worked on an assembly line or was in a management position. How a man dressed, where he lived, and the way his wife entertained were all critical factors in his success. His performance on the job was often secondary to the image he could present to the world, and his wife had to make the home a model of what the corporation viewed as a proper environment.

Church attendance was high but often for reasons other than the desire to worship God. Being seen in the right church was an image builder in the corporate world; it was good business to be an active member. The upcoming businessman avoided criticism from his neighbors, especially since everyone knew that the communist atheists might, at any moment, try to attack the suburban havens to which millions were flocking.

The need to conform and the fear of being considered different led to intense emotional stress. Although alcohol became the standard escape in suburbia, many Americans hooked themselves on the new tranquilizers. Within five years of the introduction of Miltown and Thorazine, 1.2 million pounds of pills were being prescribed for average Americans. A 1959 study of the idyllic suburban community of Englewood, New Jersey, revealed that the families were plagued with ulcers, heart attacks, and seemingly countless "tension related, psychosomatic disorders."

A second form of escape entered the lives of some Americans in the 1950s—a new religion that seemed to offer an alternative to a world out of control. It promised instant access to wealth, power, and fame. The practitioners were convinced that their lives would probably be devoid of the promise of America, if only because of the impending annihilation by Russia. Why not seek instant access to what their

18

parents had found only through a lifetime of hard work? What they did not realize was that this religion would one day permeate all aspects of society, from the entertainment world to military and political organizations. This religion was Satanism and the monsters they unleashed now survive and multiply in every part of America.

SATAN COMES TO CALIFORNIA

There is a saying in a number of industries that everything new begins in California. Although this is obviously an exaggeration, California and the entire West Coast have served as the rallying point for the misfits, the eccentrics, the loners, and in some instances, the crazies.

California has always held a mystique for Americans. Since our society evolved from the East Coast, each time a man or woman disagreed with the local government, rebelled against perceived area oppression, or just wanted to live in a manner that might not be acceptable to others, that individual moved west. At first this meant traveling from Massachusetts or Rhode Island to the Ohio Valley. Then it was on to Missouri, Texas, or Arizona. Each move foreshadowed encroaching civilization until, at last, the West Coast was the last frontier for the person seeking an escape from whatever plagued his or her past.

So it was with Satanism. The East Coast had been settled by the Puritans, the Quakers, the Methodists, and numerous other Christian groups. When someone had a nontraditional or counterculture religious belief, the person usually had to move west to find freedom. The Mormons went to Utah, and Satanism got its first contemporary foothold in Southern California in the 1950s.

At that time California resembled a Norman Rockwell painting—large old houses on sprawling lots, front porches with white-painted swings and wicker rocking chairs. Everywhere children were jumping rope and playing hopscotch, teenagers were teasing one another as they experienced their first sexual awakenings, and the elderly were contemplating the passing parade of friends, neighbors, and seasons. Shade trees and quality construction ensured that even when a thoughtless youth had music blaring in the family's living room, a passerby would hear nothing louder than the robins chirping in tree branches overhead.

This quiet isolation of the Southern California community was why the Cambridge family so enjoyed their home. It was the perfect place to properly raise their little daughter Heather. No one would intrude on their private family activities. No one would ever hear their daughter's screams.

NEARER MY SATAN TO THEE

Alan Cambridge had always been a frightened young man. He was the high school loser, the boy who seemed to get lost in the crowd. Good looking, but not particularly athletic or popular, he had few friends and even less interest in extracurricular activities.

Perhaps a part of the problem was where Alan was raised. While most of America had experienced World War II as a distant horror, a nightmare confined to Germany, Japan, Italy, France, and other distant lands, Californians were certain that they would soon be on the front lines of combat. The Japanese had attacked Pearl Harbor. Their next destination might be Los Angeles, San Diego, or some other coastal city. Hadn't submarines already been spotted? Hadn't Japanese Americans been removed from their homes and placed in concentration camps in the Southwest to avoid an internal terrorist network that would sabotage the shipping industry?

The U.S. government established anti-air emplacements along some of the California beaches. Men too old or feeble for the draft served as Civil Defense wardens, enforcing blackouts and practicing for the air raid that might come at any moment. And the children, aware that war was imminent, recreated their versions of the blitz, the Kamikaze pilots, and frontline warfare among the rocks, the sand, and the unoccupied beachfront cottages. Sometimes a child's pointed finger was a deadly M-1 Carbine blasting a Nazi from the sky. Other times, BB guns were the weapons of the day, small boys marching solemnly by the water or firing round after round at the imaginary battleships waiting just off shore.

The games and bravado of children's play masked the fears that Alan and his friends shared about the times. He was a Catholic, his parents taking him dutifully to church where he was told of the power of God and the dangers of Satan. Yet it was during the Mass that he also witnessed the weeping women, dressed in black, praying for the souls of husbands, sons, and grandsons killed by Hitler's troops.

Alan Cambridge was shocked by the contrast between what he was hearing about a loving God and what he felt he was witnessing in church. He knew the families of the men who had died. They were good people, community leaders, regular churchgoers who went to confession, said their rosary, and kept a picture of his Holiness on their living room walls. If God wanted him to be good boy, then God should protect him from any harm. It was a simple child's faith. You receive exactly what you give, a concept that could not relate to the random, senseless violence of men at war.

The questioning continued as Alan learned more about his family's past. He discovered that his ancestors dated back to the earliest Spanish explorers and immigrants. A land grant deeded them miles of rich Southern California coastline, which brought them great wealth. They employed hundreds of laborers on their farms, lived in elegant splendor, and regularly lit candles to the saints in thanks for their many blessings. Unfortunately, they did not try to learn law or the business practices of the world that surrounded the property they owned.

The problems, when they began, were subtle for the Cambridge family. A corrupt government official would alert them to a minor debt they had somehow overlooked. The family, surprised by their failure to meet their obligations to

21

the state, would immediately make payment. They never checked to see if the debt truly existed.

Gradually the demands increased. Land had to be sold to meet the nonexistent obligations. The family felt that it would be improper to question the government. They respected authority and would not make a court challenge. Tragically, by the time that Alan was born, the family had only a large house and a few acres of land to show for their rich heritage. They no longer enjoyed the community's respect, and the remaining holdings consisted of almost worthless property.

Alan, rather withdrawn from the other children, immersed himself in a life of fantasy. He read the comic books of the era, pulp magazines whose artists created overwhelmingly terrifying, incomprehensible horrors. Numerous publications bearing such names as *Voodoo*, *Uncanny Tales*, and *Web of Mystery*, introduced blood, guts, and perversion at a price every child could afford. For a dime, one could read about encounters with the walking dead, mirrors that reflected the ugliness of a man's soul, ghouls dining on corpses, and countless other horrors. Twenty million of these ten-cent nightmares found their way into the hands of children every month before state legislators began passing the laws banning them from the stores.

Whether or not the comics had an adverse effect on the children of America was a topic of endless controversy in books and on radio. However, Alan was one youth who was influenced by such reading matter. For him, the concept of powers that could distort the lives of others was very real. He became convinced that if he could find a way to tap into the "other world," he could be someone special. He could control his own destiny and none of the forces of the universe could stop him.

The ideas that were going through Alan's head were not that much different from some of the concepts that dominated adult life in the 1950s. Many families took delight in predicting the future through the occult game known as Ouija. Thousands of copies of the book *The Search For Bridey Murphy* were purchased, turning the name of a Colorado housewife, Ruth Simmons, into a household word. She had been age regressed by amateur hypnotist Morey Bernstein; and, together, they discovered that during a previous lifetime she had been Bridey Murphy, an Irish lass with a rich brogue. The truth eventually proved to be otherwise, but that did not stop the creation of come-as-you-were parties and Reincarnation Cocktails. There were even a number of suicides by the curious who decided they wanted to experience their next life sooner than God intended.

A few of Alan's schoolmates did not think of religion, power, the future, or anything other than rebellion. They joined the teenage gangs who were sweeping the country, all sharing the same distinctive hairstyles and manner of dress. Girls wore poodle cuts, close cropped and kinky. Boys combed their hair in a style politely called a "DA." Gangs with switchblades, black leather jackets, and motorcycles saw themselves in an "us versus them" war of the "hot-rodders" against the "squares."

Some of the rebels led a Bohemian life style. They shared poetry, protest songs, and marijuana cigarettes. The women wore long hair, leotards, no lipstick, and layers of eye shadow. The men wore beards, short hair, and serious expressions. Khaki pants, sandals, and sweaters formed the rebels' equivalent of the Ivy League look.

In northern California, the men and women who would come to be known as the "Beat Generation" often traveled to San Francisco, a community that embraced eccentrics. Coffee houses seemed more numerous than gas stations. At night, the air was filled with the cacophonous blending of traffic noise, the harangues of anarchist poets shouting their latest creative efforts to passing pedestrians, and the lilt of Southern black blues songs sung by ardent white men originally from Cleveland, Chicago, and New York.

23

Southern California had a different breed of rebel. This was the land of instant power, fame, and success. The contrast between the rich and the merely comfortable was so great that owning last year's sports car was often perceived as a sign of poverty. Frustrations could be greater for a child growing up in this part of the country than perhaps anywhere else in the United States.

For easterners, the gently flowing ocean waves, sandy beaches, and year-round sunshine seemed to create a community of peace, free from the tensions of the major cities. But the contrasts of great wealth and average incomes, movie star mansions and tract houses, Rolls-Royce convertibles and Nash Ramblers, made the locals desperate for immediate change. The worry about the bomb, the economy, and even whether or not there would be a tomorrow made instant gratification an obsession.

Alan Cambridge was as obsessed with unrealistic desires as the adults around him, but his obsession never took the form of outright rebellion. His hair was kept properly short, his manner quiet, unassuming, but his mind was filled with fantasy. He was determined to learn the secrets of life that would give him power over others.

At first Alan reacted like many boys. In the back of a comic book, he read an advertisement for a martial arts course. He sent for the karate instruction, teaching himself the "Dance of Death," an impressive sounding series of movements considered a joke by serious students in the field. Then, armed with this special knowledge, he joined the army right out of high school. However, after only a few weeks in basic training, Alan Cambridge was dishonorably discharged. Even with the Korean War and the American military in need of potential cannon fodder, Cambridge was found to be unacceptable.

Alan Cambridge returned home a loser, a joke to his former friends, a man who was frustrated, angry, humiliated, and determined to find a quick way to success. He did not care if the path he chose might lead to murder, madness, and the ritualistic tortures of the damned. He did not know that he would unknowingly be sharing his deviant's journey with would-be movie stars, rock singers, doctors, lawyers, and many others. He did not realize that he was in the vanguard of a secret California religious underworld that permeated television, motion pictures, and the record industry.

It is not known just when Alan Cambridge began making his secret visits to the Haitian settlements near his southern California home. They may have begun as the result of dares from friends or after his military debacle. Whatever the case, he began sneaking into the Haitian ghettos to observe the rumored voodoo rites.

The immigrants of the ghettos of Southern California were divided into two types. Although all had poor or oppressed backgrounds and were looking for new opportunities, the less educated often worked the farm lands, picking crops, while others found jobs on estates and in private homes, working as gardeners, maids, and caretakers.

Some of the refugees were determined to assimilate, learning the language, saving their money, educating their children, and moving to nicer, integrated middle-income communities. These people lived in the ghettos but worked to become a part of the surrounding culture.

A few of the immigrants wanted nothing to do with the community at large. They formed a closed society, retaining their language, their superstitions, and a constant distrust of those in the surrounding areas. Often they were ridiculed for being different, a situation that made them angry and determined to gain revenge. Their world was a combination of fear, hate, and magic, all of which increased their separation from the greater society. The idea that a teenage boy whose California heritage stretched back many generations might come among them was exceedingly unusual.

How Alan was able to enter the ghetto sections where voodoo and other corrupted religious rites were practiced is unknown. Perhaps the area residents were amused by his

25

curiosity, or they may have sensed some of their own emotions in this angry, troubled youth. Whatever the case, he was allowed to see the specially painted signs, the secret chantings, the foul-smelling liquids prepared according to intricate recipes handed down from family to family, and the ritual slaughter of animals. He met witch doctors dressed in white and viewed altars to the saints whose presence was meant to give magical protection from punishment.

What Alan was absorbing during these visits might have been called voodoo, Devil worship, or Satanism, and it held the promise of power, wealth, and carnal delight. Within the rebellious practices was the foundation for obtaining everything he had ever desired. The fact that the people who were practicing these black arts were frightened, poverty stricken, and unable to be accepted by the surrounding world never entered his conscious awareness. Alan Cambridge decided to sell his soul to Satan.

DEVIL LORE: FRENCH FIRST BUT NOT LAST

To understand the beliefs of Alan Cambridge, convictions that would eventually lead to child abuse, incest, drugs, and murder, it is important to briefly review the origins of Satan worship. An understanding of this history is usually unimportant to the average practitioner of the black arts. He or she is seeking selfish ends that seem unattainable through the worship of a loving God. But knowing the history helps us to see how seemingly normal people, often among the educated elite, can be seduced into the blasphemous, the obscene, and the deadly by their personal desires.

DRUIDS AND OTHER DEVILMEN

Throughout recorded history, the greatest plagues we have been forced to endure have been the result of our inhumanity to one another. Illness, starvation, natural disasters, and similar afflictions have never caused the pain we have deliberately created for each other in the name of religion, politics, or vengeance.

Sometimes ritual violence has been officially condoned as the just and proper law of the land by both political and religious leaders. An honest, moral individual could be tortured without showing physical evidence of that abuse. Thus, it was once considered perfectly proper to take the arm of a man or woman accused of witchcraft and thrust it into scalding water. A tight bandage would be wrapped around the horribly burned skin for three days; then the judge removed the bandage to check the skin. If there was no evidence of disfigurement from the water torture, the people would rejoice. If the arm remained red, sore, and tender, the person was obviously guilty and had to be put to death.

The public never openly questioned such torture but blindly accepted the supposed wisdom of the clergy and judges. The fact that the justices might love killing more than seeking the truth was never mentioned.

Some ritual tortures had their beginnings in what is now France. For over two thousand years, men and women secretly gathered in caves and other hiding places throughout France in order to learn the secrets of the occult, astrology, the interpretation of omens, and similar mystical knowledge. Some of the practitioners were the forerunners of our scientists and religious leaders, people who were curious about the mysteries of the universe. Other members of the groups were psychopathic killers, deranged rapists, and the mentally disturbed who enjoyed being allowed to inflict pain in the name of religion.

The earliest written records of the perverse religious activities in the area that is now France date back to approximately three hundred years before Christ. By the time Julius Caesar led his armies through the land, human sacrifice had become an acceptable religious rite. The occasional reformer of the day, determined to stop what he felt was inhumanity, was reminded that such sacrifice was necessary. The leaders were able to tell the future by careful study of the entrails of both freshly killed humans and animals. Obviously the gods blessed such sacrifices or they never would have used the dead as a means of revealing the future.

The priests who practiced what today would be called witchcraft were known as Druids. Their order was either feared or tolerated, depending upon the period of history. By A.D. 500, government leaders were willing to allow the Druids and their followers to practice their beliefs, punishing them only for the actions that hurt others. Murder by witchcraft was punishable by death, but someone who merely caused harm to another might be punished with only a fine, a beating, and/or being placed into slavery. The Christian church would add an additional punishment by publicly excommunicating the offender if he or she had previously professed to also be a Christian.

The public began to accept witchcraft as a creation of the government when the accusation of practicing such black arts began to be used as an attack against political enemies. Queen Fredegonde (A.D. 578) lost her son to dysentery, a common ailment of the time. The dehydration resulting from the disease frequently led to death, and many lost their lives to it. However, the death conveniently happened at the time when members of the court were anxious to destroy the growing power of an army general. He was accused of having used witchcraft to kill the prince.

Proof of the general's use of witchcraft was easy to obtain. Several men and women were arrested as material witnesses. They were from among the peasants and of no consequence to the queen. To ensure their honesty, the peasants were burned, stretched on a wheel until their bones were literally pulled apart, and/or dunked under water slowly enough to obtain a confession. All were promised that they could live if they told the truth. Everyone understood that truth meant a story saying that the general was a witch, and, naturally, they all complied. They did not realize that, to avoid a possible scandal later, all of them would be killed after confessing.

The general was sentenced to death but not before he was also tortured. Since this was a fair and honorable trial by the government, hot pincers were used to rip the fingernails and toenails from his flesh. He was also slashed about the genitals and other sensitive portions of his body. The shock and extreme physical abuse led to his death even before a formal beheading could be accomplished.

The more extreme the government became in using torture on the peasants in the name of saving the country from witches, the greater the sympathy the practitioners of the black arts received. Nothing could be worse than the excesses of the government, all of which were approved by most of the church leaders. So many innocent people were torn apart in the name of justice that all accusations were considered to be fraudulent until proven otherwise. As a result, the ancestors of the early Druids, who were still practicing ritual sacrifice, the making of magic potions, and similar actions, remained hidden. They were protected by the same peasants who would have feared them had the government been less zealous in using equally horrible methods to maintain popular support.

Talk of witchcraft increased as the year A.D. 1000 approached. It was believed that this year would be the time of the last judgment for Christians. As the date drew near, the powers of evil would gain in strength, bringing violence, pestilence, horrible storms, floods, and other disasters to the people. The suffering would be the "last hurrah" for Satan. He would lash out at the world, showing his strength, taking as many lives and souls as he could, before Christ returned.

The Christians had no idea what to expect as the end of the first millennium after Christ approached. Working seemed foolish, so many of them left their jobs, sold their possessions, and made the trek to Jerusalem where the Lord was to reign. Many buildings went unrepaired because there would be more glorious housing awaiting their occupants. Royalty abandoned their wealth; farmers stopped working the land; and everyone kept an eye on the heavens, awaiting the return of the Son of God and the banishment of the Antichrist.

The impending joy was coupled with great fear. For almost a century, the people anticipated the coming of Christ, constantly aware that Satan would be stronger than ever in their midst. Repressive legislation was passed to destroy witches, and a man or woman could be burned at the stake if there was even the suspicion of witchcraft. Jews were added to the list of the evil ones, and many lost their lives in the frenzy to protect the earth from the Antichrist. Each thunderstorm, each flash of lightning could create fear among the people. Was it Christ? Was it Satan? Or was it a natural event, unrelated to the Second Coming?

Time passed and Christ did not return. The one thousand years was obviously in error. The church had to rethink its position; people had to restore their lives; and governments were in turmoil, resorting to holy crusades and military campaigns to expand or defend territory.

Stories of witchcraft diminished; black arts were not practiced enough for the people to be particularly concerned. Calling someone a sorcerer was no longer a guaranteed method for eliminating that person as a rival. However, it was during this period that some of the beliefs that would ultimately mold the perverted world of Alan Cambridge began to take shape.

Perhaps the most important concept was the idea that demons could have sexual intercourse with humans. In 1275, for example, a French woman named Angele de la Barthe reflected upon her past. She said she had enjoyed sex with demons and had even given birth to a monster in this way. She admitted to using infants to feed this monster child of hers, murdering some of the infants and obtaining others from freshly dug graves.

Many men who would eventually attain sainthood, including Saint Thomas Aquinas and Saint Bonaventura, discussed

31

the matter of intercourse between demons and humans. They believed that the demon could enter the body of a human and use that body as a vehicle for having sex with an innocent. It was a concept modern day Satanists embraced with fervor because it meant guiltless desires. Even incest could not be taboo so long as the person forcing the sex was possessed by a demon.

THE KNIGHTS TEMPLAR

The first link between the rituals Alan Cambridge learned from the voodoo practices and the older French rites came with the Knights Templar, a religious order supposedly loyal to the pope. The Knights Templar evolved from the desire of some military men to follow noble ideals in 1118. Jerusalem, the holy city for a number of different religious groups, was under the control of the Mohammedans. The Crusaders, knights dedicated to the Catholic church, freed the city from Mohammedan rule so that the Christians could control the area.

Hugues de Payens and Geoffrey de St. Omer were French knights who had fought to free Jerusalem during the Crusades and recognized that their work was only partially completed. They decided to form a religious order that would be loyal to the pope and dedicated to protecting the pilgrims traveling to and from the Holy Land. The order would consist of men who were willing to devote their lives to this noble cause. They would serve as a form of city police offering an escort for Christians threatened by the Mohammedans.

The rules for Knights Templar membership were rigid and the men who took the vows were greatly respected. They wore white robes with red crosses. They divided themselves into work categories, ranging from a mounted army to a division providing spiritual leadership for the other Knights Templar members.

During the following centuries, the Knights Templar gradually became demoralized and corrupted. They lost faith in the

Catholic church; they wanted wealth, fame, and glory, none of which seemed to come from serving pilgrims. A number of the members decided that the answer was to look to the "opposition." If worshiping God failed to help them reach their desires, perhaps Satan would be more responsible. Their ceremonies would be on the same date as those of the Catholic church, but they would reverse all the rituals.

In 1307, approximately three hundred years after the Knights Templar's founding, an investigation revealed that members engaged in strange rituals, some of which would eventually become the basis for vodoo and satanic worship. The first of these rituals was cross defilement rather than reverence. A new member was expected to spit upon, trample, and otherwise desecrate the cross.

Among the other activities expected of the rebels within the Knights Templar were acts in opposition to biblical and Catholic teachings. These included the worship of idols shaped in the form of a man's head, the omission of parts of the Catholic Mass, and the use of laymen to grant absolution of sins. The members, both homosexual and heterosexual, were also expected to engage in sodomy.

The Knights Templar did not believe that Christ was the son of God, but rather an imposter who deserved their contempt for his fraudulent proclamations and ultimate defilement on the cross.

The Knights Templar also appeared to practice what has been called the Adamite heresy. Marriage was unknown in the Garden of Eden, and nudity was the proper state for humans, according to these believers. Sensuality was everything, and the followers felt themselves exempt from all moral laws. Their actions were meant to show their contempt for the Catholic church, engaging in whatever conduct would be considered sinful or taboo by the pope and priests.

The Adamites were to appear later, including in California. In 1925, a woman named Anna Rhodes declared herself the leader of one such group in the tiny community of Oroville.

She claimed to be Eve reincarnated, her husband being Adam, and a number of people believed them. They liked to dance in the nude and physically brand their followers during a fire ceremony, an action so painful that it led to at least one death. They also ritualistically slaughtered and/or engaged in sex acts with animals. Although this group was not active by the 1950s, some of their rites were similar to the voodoo acts Alan Cambridge studied.

ONE NATION UNDER SATAN

During the fifteenth century, France was in turmoil; people were rebelling against both the church and the government. The pope in Rome had approved the use of inquisitors to torture citizens to learn whatever truth was desired at the moment. Many innocent peasants suffered painful deaths during the search for witches, heretics, rebels, and others. The men and women who truly stood against the established order went underground, meeting secretly and establishing their own rituals in opposition to the Catholic church.

The Black Mass was ritualized so that there could be conformity among the groups. Each celebration and every holiday of the Catholic church was obscenely reversed. Men and women urinated in the Communion chalice. Naked women were used as altars. The cross was hung upside down and often trampled upon. Catholic holy days were mocked by a joyous celebration of life on Good Friday, the day Christ died, and by a ritual murdering of animals or, it was rumored, people, on Easter Sunday when Christ rose from the dead.

Many of the Catholics combined their church teachings with the "magical" acts of Devil worship. The peasants were often isolated from one another on farmlands, so they created fantasy creatures of the night to scare one another, much like Scouts today invent ghosts around the campfire.

For example, one belief back then was in the spirit of death, a humanlike figure named Ankon. Naturally, for impact, it was said that Ankon only traveled after dark. He would call on

34

people inside their homes, bidding them out to the street if it was their time to die. The people would pray in the Catholic church, believe in the Bible, yet they would spend their nights in fear of Ankon's voice.

Numerous other myths abounded, many with their origins in the early Druid teachings. Men who liked to catch and ride wild horses feared the evil creature Mouriche. This was a demon who appeared in the form of a year-old colt. A youth unexpectedly mounting Mouriche, which looked like any other wild horse needing to be tamed, would experience the last ride he or she would ever take. You could not dismount or be thrown from Mouriche. Your body was bonded to that of the demon, and your ride would take you straight to hell. No one ever witnessed such a horror, of course, but everyone knew of a "friend of a friend" who mounted a colt in play and ended in the flaming world of Satan.

It was in those times and among such people that many forms of satanic worship developed. Voodoo began in France with peasants combining concepts from the Knights Templar, the Catholic church, and remnants of the Druid teachings. They followed the priests, read the Bible, then obtained potions and powders to help them, just in case. Others openly embraced the Devil, joining the small cult meetings in an effort for power and wealth beyond even the greatest dreams of the rich land owners.

Eventually Satan worship reached the upper class of France. Many of the wealthy lived in castles where they could indulge in any behavior they desired without being detected. Their actions usually involved children, combining the most obscene aspects of child molestation, sadism, and necrophilia.

The children of servants could easily be enticed away from their homes, having no fear of the estate owners. When such a man talked with the children, their parents were flattered to see the rich, highborn owner with his arm around one of their sons or daughters, guiding the child into the forest. Surely the wealthy could mean no harm. And when the children failed to return, the parents were comforted by the fact that the landowner would occasionally participate in the search.

The true fate of these children was horrible. Girls were often bound to altars for torture and rape. Sodomy was practiced on small boys, the orgasm followed by strangulation. No matter what ritual was performed, no matter how the child was put to death, a knife was immediately plunged into the body so the still warm heart could be removed.

The exact number of children put to death in these rituals is unknown. Facts frequently were mingled with sensational rumors, yet the truth was frightening enough. During one eight-year period, enough records were maintained so that it is certain that at least eight hundred children were ritualistically put to death, their bodies either burned or buried.

Slowly the people rebelled against the highborn murderers. Investigations revealed the identities of some of the participants in the ritual slaughters honoring Satan. A few were repentant, eventually going insane from guilt or using their money to create buildings for the public good. Others were proud to be put to death, convinced that they would be granted immortality for their loyalty to Satan. Still others went undetected, a constant source of fear among the people since children continued to disappear.

Gradually satanic practice took consistent forms. Ceremonies evolved for the celebration of life and the ritual slaughter of the innocent. All Saints Day, a time roughly corresponding to our present celebration of Halloween, was a festival in which a child must die. Easter Sunday also required a sacrifice to counter the Catholic church's joy in the resurrection of Christ. There were also celebrations during the summer and winter solstices.

Sex acts of all manner had to be performed by the cult members. Rituals required that human and animal blood be tasted by the participants. When a human was put to death, the still warm heart had to be removed. Dogs were used to eat some of the human organs following this sacrifice. Perversion

36

after perversion became ritual in a religion as structured as that which was practiced within the church.

The priests softened in their hatred of the Devil worshipers by the time the seventeenth century began. Exorcism had become an established rite of the church. It was difficult to believe that any humans could voluntarily stoop to the levels of evil being reported among the Satan worshipers. Instead, it was decided that they were acting against their wills; they had somehow been lax in their religious practices, laying themselves open to possession. They were under the control of Satan rather than voluntarily indulging in the obscene practices. Special prayer services had to be devised to relieve some of the evil that possessed them. When the exorcisms were successful, the men and women were allowed to live, often entering monastic lives that would isolate them from the public. The occasional Satanist who was put to death was usually the leader of the cult.

Perhaps the greatest perversion developing during this period was the use of infants for the ceremonies. Pregnant women were encouraged to turn their babies over to Satan. Those who agreed went to the cult at the first signs of labor. The newborn children were crucified on tiny crosses. Often hosts, the unleavened bread wafers serving as the symbolic body of Christ, were nailed into the infants as well. If any of the participants were sickened by the sight of those agonizing deaths, they, too, were killed.

Once again the public was outraged by the satanic acts that were leaving trails of death and torture. No one was safe from the possibility of being kidnapped and killed, whether they be an innocent child or a virtuous older person.

Despite the trials, vigilante groups, and other pressures brought against those suspected of satanic practices, many of the cult members stayed in France, conducting their rituals in secret; but many others decided to leave the country.

INTO ALL THE WORLD

Settlements in North and South America were being widely publicized as havens for the cult members—areas where people could commit their atrocities unimpeded by those around them.

Eventually the satanic practices mingled with the Catholic missionary teachings in Haiti, Cuba, and elsewhere. Voodoo, Satan worship, and other activities related to Devil worship took hold among both the rich and poor of South America. And when these people were forced from their homes for the same reasons their ancestors had been run out of France, many of them migrated to Southern California.

It was this history of blood perversion to which Alan Cambridge was introduced in the early 1950s. He was not an intellectual who had read the writings of men such as Aleister Crowley, one of the twentieth century writers and proponents of Satanism. His exposure was to people who had bastardized religion and promoted superstition and fear. For the first time in his lonely, unsuccessful life, he saw a way to be magically transformed into a person with sex appeal, power, and wealth. All he had to do was embrace Satan, an action that would put him in the vanguard of the cult fervor, which would affect even the rich and famous on the west coast. And the only price he would have to pay would be the life of his daughter, Heather, who was destined to become the bride of Satan.

DEVILS ON HORSEBACK

DEVIL-BRIDE: HEATHER CAMBRIDGE

She was a beautiful infant, a rosy-cheeked little blond who might have been the delight of any family. She was born at the end of January, a time when Southern California is particularly pleasant, yet Alan Cambridge convinced his wife that caring for the child without any help would be difficult for her. It was important to hire someone to help, even though the addition of a part-time nursemaid would be an extravagance the young couple could not afford. What he did not say was that he had calculated the time of birth, the number of days from the satanic New Year (January 13), and come to the conclusion that Heather Cambridge was the preordained bride of Satan. During the next twenty-eight years, it would be Alan's job to ensure that she was properly prepared to return to "the father who art in hell."

The nursemaid retained by the Cambridge family was a woman of Haitian descent and a practitioner of witchcraft. He wanted her to help him learn the black arts, to utilize his special child for his own ends. Together they would prepare Heather for her destiny.

A MAN AFTER SATAN'S OWN HEART

The events Heather later remembered sound like the nightmares of the damned. They are difficult to believe, even for those adults who have viewed the results of extreme child abuse, yet medical testimony from several complete physical examinations confirms the fact that Heather experienced more brutality than can be easily described.

The horrors began with the rape of the infant using a variety of blunt instruments, including a small crucifix. As Heather grew older and attempted to resist, she was bound to an altar for the ritual tortures, which then included the dripping of hot wax as a way of cleansing her skin. And always the violence was conducted while her father read the Bible to her, reciting endless verses to justify his actions.

"It was 'family night' every Friday," Heather recalls. "My father would take out the Bible, and it was as if he had gone into a trance. Sometimes he would read from it, but usually he would be saying nonsense. Everybody was on drugs, and they would listen to him as though he was making sense. He was talking nonsense, but I was the only one who knew it."

Heather's mother was not a participant in the violence, though it is unknown how much she knew. She encouraged Heather to visit her father after the divorce, and Heather always returned home battered. It was as though no one wanted to face what might be happening.

No organized satanic worship in Southern California existed when Alan Cambridge began his ritual violence against his daughter. This did not matter to him, though, because his concern was gaining power and success. Once he had learned all the possible voodoo from his nursemaid, he dismissed her and began experimenting with drugs. He used marijuana, then difficult to obtain, and other mind-altering chemicals in an effort to achieve even greater sensual experiences. He also began talking about his satanic beliefs in bars and other places where he thought he could do so without getting into trouble. From such efforts he gradually gathered the names of like-minded men and women.

At the same time that Alan Cambridge was developing his own cult, he worked in a variety of jobs. He was a printer for a while, apparently quite skilled at his work, and experimented with counterfeiting money, an action that led to one of his earliest arrests. He also claimed to still be a part of the military, secretly working for the Criminal Intelligence Division, a statement that seems to have no basis in fact. However, since his wife had family in the South, he often used his "military activities" as an excuse for leaving his wife, daughter, and, later, their sons, with his mother-in-law while he ostensibly went to some of the bases. From arrest records pieced together over the years, it is more likely that he consorted with drug dealers who sold to soldiers on the base, drank, and got high.

Cambridge was a handsome man in his early years, and he had the burning intensity and gift of gab that have made other cult leaders so successful. He promised new sensual and religious experiences. He offered power and he instilled fear in those who might otherwise have stood against him.

Gradually Alan Cambridge's followers increased in numbers. Betty, a girl in her late teens, who was an immoral misfit interested in drugs, sex, and power, eventually became Alan's chief assistant, his lover, and his second wife. She would also serve time in jail in Mexico and allegedly took part in one or more human sacrifices.

LuAnne, another member of the group, was extremely intelligent, interested in new philosophies, and scared of the times. Cambridge's satanic cult offered her a chance to belong to a group that offered her instant gratification of her desires. She came to realize the falseness of the group's promises and the violence of its actions, so she left the group, returned to college, and became seriously involved in Christianity.

Other members had widely varying backgrounds from airline pilot to medical professional. Some sought success and sensual pleasure; others had become "burned out on God" and decided that maybe Satanism had some answers for them.

Whatever the reasons for joining, Alan Cambridge knew just how far he could manipulate his group. During the weekly ritual tortures of Heather, only two of his closest women followers were ever present, and they either accepted or enjoyed the violence against the child. They would sit in a darkened room, place lighted black candles in a symbolic order, and begin "studying" the Bible. Alan would do the reading, sometimes quoting the Scriptures exactly but more frequently speaking gibberish in a hypnotic state as he stared at the burning wax. Although the two women thought the messages were from Hell, Heather, when old enough to read, recognized that frequently her father was holding the Bible upside down and that was the reason for the incomprehensible words. Only once did she dare question what he was doing, a questioning that resulted in so violent a beating that she never dared argue with his drug-induced logic again.

With little Satanic activity on a national scale during those early years, it was not until 1966, when Heather was twelve years old, that Anton LaVey of San Francisco shaved his head, began wearing a black clerical collar, and declared himself the founder of the Church of Satan. LaVey's group gained massive international attention and became the standard against which Alan Cambridge's cult judged itself. The members felt that LaVey was Satan's representative on earth and, from that day forward, they sought to act in a manner they felt would gain his approval. The fact that LaVey did not know Cambridge, nor would likely have condoned the actions of Alan's cult, was not a concern to the members.

The size of the Cambridge cult was never known and may have varied over the years. Typically nine to thirteen members came to the major rituals. Betty, the priestess who served as the co-leader, temple prostitute, and girlfriend of Cambridge, always dressed in red. She eventually married Alan when Heather was ten, the couple living near his ex-wife so they could maintain weekly visits with the child. Alan's ex-wife was delighted to have Alan retain such a strong, "healthy" interest in their daughter and never considered denying him visitation privileges.

A LIVING SACRIFICE

The weekly ritual of violence often left young Heather visibly bruised. Early school pictures show her with swollen eyes and mottled cheeks from the obvious beatings. Yet neither school teachers nor neighbors chose to get involved. They did not want to question what was taking place in the home. Child abuse was still an issue that was not discussed. The home was sacred and what went on behind closed doors was considered a family matter. Parents knew best, a theme echoed on television; and even young Heather, when talking with her girlfriends, was shocked to learn that other parents did not cause their children physical pain. She had come to accept the abuse as a natural part of growing up and was inwardly proud that she no longer had to be held down for the tortures. She had developed enough self-control to endure the pain without screaming or resisting. She had become a survivor.

Many of the ceremonies were designed to convince Heather that there were two sides to her, a good side for all the world to see and a satanic side that evolved from the nature of her birth. Alan Cambridge had learned hypnosis and through it tried to convince his daughter that she had two separate personalities. This was reinforced by cult rituals in which the members of the group would paint their faces. They would make a four-part-checkerboard pattern on their faces with makeup. They would place two black sections diagonally opposite each other and two white squares opposite each other on the other side. Then they would take pieces of clear window glass and hold them in front of their faces, telling Heather they were holding mirrors.

Betty and her father would secure Heather to an altar before the remaining members entered. Then they would move around Heather, looking closely at her through the pieces of glass while Alan Cambridge told her they were holding mirrors. She came to believe that she was seeing her own face reflected by the people. The black sections reflected Satan and the white reflected the face most people saw. She was being made to believe that there was an evil aspect to her, one only those in the know recognized, yet one that required her to constantly obey the base desires of the cult members.

There were other facets to the cult, including child sacrifice. As Heather later related to a former FBI official, now a private investigator, "It was explained to me they were children who belonged to members of the cult. The mother offered her own child up and if the mother didn't cooperate, she was killed also."

When Heather turned thirteen, one year after her father's group declared their allegiance to Anton LaVey, the ultimate nightmare took place. Heather was of age, an adult woman who could become the bride of Satan. This was a day for which the group had been planning since her birth. This was the time when Satan would enter the body of one of the male members, joining with his bride through ritual intercourse, passing on his seed to create a new life for hell.

The idea behind the ritual seems far more perverted today than it did when it was first developed approximately four centuries earlier. The 1500s was a time when disease, malnutrition, and similar problems resulted in extremely short life spans. Sexual maturity was considered adulthood because so many men and women died by the time they were thirty years of age. Thus the idea of a thirteen-year-old girl having sex was quite proper since it was time for her to begin having children and to take on the responsibilities of a family. The fact that by the 1960s a thirteen-year-old could in no way be considered a consenting adult was overlooked in the perverted reasoning of the satanic cult.

The first stages of preparation involved a cleansing shower. Betty and the other members determined that Satan would use the body of the male leader, so Alan Cambridge entered the shower with his daughter. He did not perceive his actions as being incestuous because, in his twisted mind, he was not Heather's father. His body was but a shell for Satan to use while on earth. Whatever happened between his body and Heather's was the result of Satan's actions. His touch was Satan's touch. His seed would be Satan's seed.

As Heather later related to an investigator, "Sometimes he said he *was* Satan. Other times he just attributed those titles to himself. He believed that Satan would enter his body. And in that respect he was Satan, but he would qualify that and say he knew that he was just a vessel for Satan, much in the same way that Christians say 'I am a vessel for the Lord.'"

Following the shower, Betty and one of the other female members carefully dried, powdered, and dressed Heather in a beautiful white gown. She had long been prepared through sexual abuse and torture. Now her battered body was considered properly pure for the ritual to come, and she was laid upon the altar. Ten more members of the cult joined the three leaders, and eerie, dissonant music was played in the background. Only the candles supplied illumination.

The specifics of the ceremony are not remembered by those participants who have been willing to talk; but Alan Cambridge did have intercourse with his daughter during the ritual, and both he and his followers were convinced that Satan was the one having the sexual relationship.

CHILD OF CALAMITY

Heather Cambridge became pregnant. The torture ended, but the group stayed close to her, keeping aware of her every activity, making their presence known in her life.

It is not known why the pregnancy was not noticed by

others. One possibility is that Heather was enough overweight that her body did not obviously show the pregnancy. Another possibility is that teachers and others who saw her assumed that a thirteen-year-old girl would not be pregnant and just ignored what they saw. Since Heather was a loner and sexual promiscuity among teens was still a rarity, no one considered the possibility that her father may have raped her in the name of Satan.

What happened next is uncertain. It is believed that a cult member who worked in a hospital took instruments and emergency oxygen equipment to an isolated canyon area a few miles from Alan's home. A baby boy was delivered during a satanic ceremony; however, the child was either born dead or was killed immediately after birth because it was "defective" in some way. Then the group held a blood ceremony in perverted celebration of the experience.

"I was shown something that looked like a fetus," said Heather. "I was laid on a table, my legs in a birthing position. I couldn't see what was going on. I experienced quite a lot of pain. I had a lot of cramping. They had surgical-looking tools, and they were hurting me in the genital area. After all this pain, blood, and such, I was pretty worn out, emotionally, psychologically, and physically. I was shown this bloody thing and told that it was a fetus."

The trauma of the ritual childbirth and the shock of the baby's death were overwhelming for Heather. She became seriously ill and had to be nursed for several days following the ceremony. She was kept in her father's house with Betty acting as the primary caretaker during this difficult period. No mention of the birth or the ceremony was made. No rituals were performed. All symbols and books related to the satanic activities were hidden from her view. It was as though she had entered a quiet country home in order to convalesce from a long illness; the evil intentions that had come so close to causing her death perhaps never had existed.

The cult frequently used animals for sacrifices. As Heather

explained, "Obviously you can't just sacrifice a human every time you have a ritual, because that would eventually expose that group. More often than not, their sacrifice involved small animals. During the time in which my father had me, he would get pets. I would be told they were my pets. Later when it came time for them to be sacrificed, I was made to believe that I had done something wrong again, and for punishment, this animal of mine had to be cruelly tortured and put to a horrible death.

"I always felt responsible. I felt if I had just been a better girl, or just good enough, they would stop the killing and torturing of animals and they wouldn't hurt any more people. Invariably, in each case, I was made to believe that it was because of me and because I wasn't good enough that these things had to happen; so I constantly strived to be as good as I could, but I never was good enough."

Heather indicated that human and animal sacrifices were generally kept separate from each other, and that even animals were not sacrificed every time they got together.

The gatherings were once or twice a week, but the sacrifices of any sort were far less frequent. The animal sacrifices would often be completed for their own sake. However, she said her father told her that animal sacrifices also preceded human sacrifice. "The animal blood was sprinkled on the person before and after their death. They tried to get cats. Little kittens are easiest to get a hold of. The cat's throat is slit. That was the way I usually saw them killed, with throat slit, and then blood is sprinkled. Sometimes I was aware of a situation where they were angry at somebody, but they didn't kill this person. What they would do is go sprinkle blood on that person's doorstep as some sort of a warning.

"According to what I learned from my father, if there was some death and it could be traced to cult activity, it was probably a death where they caused an accident. They didn't actually have this person and kill them during a ritual. Later they would go and sprinkle blood on the grave and then leave some sign, generally something to do with the number 13. It could be anything. They could leave 13 blades of grass stuck together. They could leave 13 small stones. That number 13 is their way of leaving a mark, and as far as I know, that is common to all satanic cults in the United States. It was not an act peculiar to my father's cult."

As to the differences between an animal and a human sacrifice, Heather stated:

> The way it was explained to me is when a human is sacrificed, they would cut the heart out. As far as an animal being sacrificed, when the animal was being killed, it was horribly tortured—of course, the human was, too—but the animal's throat was slit and then the entrails were taken out and members of the cult would drink the blood of the animal and sometimes eat part of the entrails or the heart.
>
> In the human, the heart was taken out, and in the cupped hands of whomever was leading the ceremony, it was raised up. It seems like a perverse, mirror-image of the Catholic Mass in which the priest takes the Eucharist which is the body of Christ and raises it up towards heaven, as an offering. In that same manner, the leader of the cult raises the human heart up.

Satanism is in some ways a perverse mirror image of the Catholic Church.

UNFAMILIAR FACES

The psychological damage to Heather was intense. She developed what psychiatrists call hysteric dissociation or, more commonly, a multiple personality. One personality existed to endure whatever tortures the cult might want to inflict upon her body. A second personality, the satanic side, was angry and violent, approving the tortures and the sacrifices. A third personality was a perfect child, good in school, polite to adults, a front used to deny the horrors of her secret life.

One personality became that of a prostitute so Heather could earn enough money to live away from home. Another was a small child, apparently the "original" Heather before the violence was inflicted. And yet another had but one purpose, to keep the body alive for another 15 years, at which time she would be ritualistically murdered so that she could join her husband, Satan, in hell for all eternity.

Eventually Heather left home, staying in Southern California, keeping in contact with her father's cult, but no longer being victimized by them. She entered college, took jobs, and made friends with other young men and women, none of whom were aware of the intense violence she had endured.

At times she suppressed memories from the past until a series of suicidal urges led her to seek emotional help. Then, in the psychologist's office, she felt safe enough to tell a little about her past.

She revealed violence beyond imagination. She told about one time when the cult discovered a spy in their midst, apparently a would-be writer who felt that infiltrating the group would be his key to fame. He was not employed by a news organization and did not have family in the area where the cult operated. When they discovered what he was doing, he was taken to a canyon area to be tortured to death.

The death described by Heather, who had been forced to witness it, was sickeningly brutal. First, he was bound and suspended upside down from a tree. Then his vocal cords were severed, he was blinded, and his tongue slashed. Finally numerous cuts were made on his body until the blood loss, pain, and shock killed him. Eventually the body was removed and dumped in the vast canyon area where discovery was highly unlikely.

Other stories included tales of animal sacrifice. Because she was frequently blindfolded she could not name the dates or the exact locations, yet the descriptions of the deaths confirmed known violence in the general area where the family was living in the 1960s. During this time Southern

California law enforcement officers were occasionally finding evidence of animal sacrifices and ritual murders. The manner of the killings seem to substantiate Heather's stories.

The information that has been obtained about Heather's family seems to support her statements. Her father had an ever growing arrest record related to drugs, alcohol abuse, and violence. Then, towards the end of 1981, Heather and those trying to help her received death threats. At the time she was twenty-seven years old, and it was time for the cult to prepare her to die on Halloween night (All Saints Eve) the following year. The preparations would take several months following her twenty-eighth birthday that January, and she was warned not to leave the state.

The death did not occur. Heather was removed from her home through the assistance of several different law enforcement agencies. She was relocated to a different state, receiving both physical protection and intense counseling.

A TANGLED WEB

How important is Heather Cambridge? How unique? How accurate is her story?

The answers are hard to know. As much as she hated her life, as badly as she was hurt, the child abuse was all she knew. No information could be compared with friends because Satanist activities were never discussed outside the home. It was only as an adult that she faced her uniqueness as a victim.

Incest therapists occasionally tell stories about adults who, as children, were ritualistically abused. In therapy these adults talk about Satan worship, though their numbers are few relative to the total number of adults who were abused as children.

Police departments sometimes hear rumors about Satanist rituals surrounding the deaths of some adult females, but they have no verification. The victim is dead and prosecutors are reluctant to bring the motive of Satan worship into a murder case for fear the jury will take it less seriously. If they can gain a conviction from the act of murder, the motives surrounding it are not always of concern during the trial.

When analyzing Heather's complete story, several factors come into play. Heather spoke of ritual tortures and rapes with screwdrivers, crucifixes, and other items, plus the cleansing ritual of scalding showers and the dripping of hot wax onto her genitals. Obviously, a physical examination should reveal some marks or scars on her body.

A physician examined Heather, knowing only that she claimed to have been a child abuse victim. When the examination was complete, he was extremely pale and nauseated. When he was able to talk, he reported on the damage he had found—body burn marks and severe vaginal scars, which he felt would be impossible to self-inflict. He also said that much of the damage was so old that it probably occurred when she was a small child.

As to the questions about murders she had witnessed, her stories, while horrible, were no different from the confessions of some Satanists to ritual murders. Heather's story about the "spy" in the group's midst fit other known torture murders. It was common for the eyes to be removed as a lesson that the victim had seen what he should not have seen, the tongue to be removed because he had spoken what should not be said, and the nose removed because it had led him into areas that were none of his business. After the death, the heart was routinely removed and consumed, along with the ritual drinking of the blood.

Yet other stories are of even greater concern. Heather spoke of being taught how to kill by her father, using as an example the deaths of Jayne Mansfield and her lover, lawyer Sam Brody.

For Heather Cambridge, the story of Jayne Mansfield was a more personal one. Her father, Alan, was delighted with the death and proudly took credit for it. He took Heather to the family car and showed her the hose that held the brake fluid.

He showed her how he had made a pinhole in the hose of Jayne's car, causing a small leak and eventually brake failure. Even though no skid marks would be found, the front-end crash would probably have destroyed the evidence of breakline tampering.

Heather wondered why her father had taken such an action. She was told that Anton Lavey, author of *The Satanic Bible*, had placed a curse on Brody and that he, Alan Cambridge, was called upon by Satan to fulfill it. In his madness, Cambridge had taken the news of the curse personally, feeling he had to act under orders he had never received. He claimed to have located the car Mansfield and Brody were using, then fixed the hose so that a crash would occur.

Were his words truthful? No one knows. Cambridge was in the New Orleans area where Mansfield and Brody died. He would have had the opportunity, the motive, and the knowledge of how to handle such a crime. Yet he was never investigated because murder was not a consideration, and any evidence that might come forth now would be too long after the crime to be conclusive.

Heather and her father also were linked to the ritual killing of the family of Jeff MacDonald, a Green Beret doctor at Fort Bragg, North Carolina, whose story is a chapter in this book. As she stated, "The people who killed his family were angry that he wouldn't cooperate as far as drug dealing—some sort of drug act.

"They wanted to get back at him [MacDonald]. I know that his wife and two little girls were killed and he wasn't. He was seriously injured. From what I gathered from my father, they initially thought they'd killed the whole family."

Heather explained that the family was supposed to die from the stabbings, that Jeff MacDonald was not supposed to live. She also implicated Helena Stoeckley, a woman who admitted to being a part of the murder, although she was never arrested or charged. Helena and Heather were stopped for questioning by Michael Furey, a police officer in the area who was concerned that Heather was in violation of the car curfew. Later, Helena would stress that for full information on the crime, they should find Heather. However, she failed to give a last name, and Helena did not know where Heather lived.

"He [Heather's father] told me that he and Helena had planned the murders [of the MacDonald family] on Halloween prior [1969]. I thought he knew MacDonald by the way he was talking. He and Helena had planned the murders; I would assume he knew MacDonald."

She explained that cult members in North Carolina participated and that Helena had been practicing Satanism and was connected with a cult. She claimed that although she was not involved, she later provided details of the case. Her testimony in time matched that of witnesses in the area, both substantiating her claims of awareness and indicating that she may have been present that night herself.

Heather did not become important until her stories were checked against other reports. In Sacramento, California, three teenage girls spoke of being physically and sexually abused by practicing Satanists. They spoke of ritual sacrifices of small children, and medical evidence indicated that they had been "cleansed" in much the same manner as Heather. Eight boys and girls between the ages of four and fifteen, all living in King County, Texas, told police that they were forced to witness two ritual homicides and eat parts of the body. Francisco Fuster Escalone of Miami, Florida, was sentenced to life in prison in October 1985, for sexually abusing children during rituals in which they were told to pray to Satan.

The stories seem endless, from Ohio, Michigan, Colorado, and elsewhere—tales of abuse, murder, and satanic wedding ceremonies. As a result of this information, we decided to explore the entire field of satanic activity in an effort to learn the types of activities occurring and, most importantly, the extent of the problem. This book is what followed, and the explorations begun by Heather Cambridge have important implications for all of us.

DEVIL-TONGUE:
TED RABOUIN

"I think anybody who gets into witchcraft has, to begin with, an extremely high supernatural curiosity," said Ted Rabouin, a former Satanist who has now returned to Christianity after running one of the most successful independent satanic groups on the east coast. "In other words, I think most of the people who do get into it are extremely religious people, but their religion doesn't pay off for them. They want another means of getting it easy. They want the good life. They are nobodies in this respect, but they don't want to go to school. They are flunkies. Extremely high egos—all of them. They have nothing and it is so easy for them to get on the radio and television by saying they are witches. That in itself makes people curious, and they get a foothold. It is the start of fame and the next thing they know they are in books and granting interviews and on stage at schools and universities."

THE HOUNDS OF HELL

Rabouin's comments may describe the leadership of many Satanist groups but not the followers. Although his background was one of poverty, hardship, and pain, the people he led were doctors, lawyers, priests, nuns, and other members of the clergy. Although uneducated in the traditional sense, Rabouin had a brilliant mind, an understanding of psychology, and a belief in his ability to tap into the dark side of life.

Rabouin was born into a low-income Catholic family and attended parochial schools with his brothers and sisters. He was also a homosexual, a child who, from at least the age of five, only remembers being attracted to males. Unlike many children with a same-sex preference, he had no history of abuse or emotional disturbance. His family was poor and loving but completely frustrated by his sexual variance.

"From the time I was very small, I remember my family and teachers telling me, 'You're such a good boy, Teddy, but you're going to hell.' I was always a 'good boy,' and I was always told I was going to hell for liking other boys."

By the time Rabouin was old enough for high school, tragedy struck. His parents were killed, and as a teenager, he was suddenly thrust into the role of parent. He loved his brothers and sisters, and determined to keep them together as a unit, he worked at every job he could find. He wanted no government intervention or foster care to separate him from his siblings. Ted became an instant adult, a nurturing father, a man-child unable to enjoy the normal activities of high school. His formal education stopped; only his avid thirst for knowledge and regular reading of a wide variety of books helped him to continue on the path of knowledge.

And always there was the criticism. Always he was a "good boy." Always he was going to hell.

Then came a love affair, a serious relationship with a somewhat older man. Rabouin was not promiscuous. He was not the type of homosexual who seeks an endless series of

58

casual sexual encounters. His feelings for the other man were as intense as any married couple who had delayed physical pleasure until after wedlock. And when this relationship ended, several years after it began, it was cancer that came between them.

The death of the lover, the years of poverty and struggle, and the constant refrain about being a good boy but going to hell, took their toll on Rabouin. He decided that God had failed him. God had made him homosexual; then he had taken the only man he ever loved. God had granted him a past in poverty, a future in hell, and a present that cost him the only love he felt he had ever had. He decided that the only sensible action would be to obtain whatever benefits he could on earth and to do that, he invoked the names of all the men who had ever gone to hell. "I reached out to Satan by calling on the names of Hitler, Bluebeard, Caligula, and every other evil man of history I could think of."

Rabouin also began studying the writings of Satanists, magicians, and practitioners of witchcraft. He felt that there had to be a formula for evil, just as the Bible provides information for those seeking to follow the ways of the Lord. He studied and experimented until he began to get results. He had no idea what was happening, what forces he was encountering, and he did not care. He left himself open to the minds of the historic Satanists, seeking to be filled with their knowledge day and night. "I said I was living in the twentieth century, and I made the romance of the Middle Ages come alive again. I crowned myself like Napoleon did on the steps of Notre Dame, and I waited for the subjects to come in awe of me—and they did."

SEDUCTIVE WORDS

When Ted Rabouin became the leader of his own satanic group, he went forth recruiting. In the guise of ecumenical understanding, he arranged to speak in Catholic churches, among other locations, and there he would create a perverted message just logical enough to be considered by those hearing it.

"If you can't get the goodies from God, get them from somewhere else," Rabouin explained when discussing how he established himself with the followers who came to him. "The actual structure [of his group] I made it as medieval as could be. I did my cellar up in paneling that looked like rocks, and each cubicle that looked like a gothic monastery. The circle was painted on the floor and there were torch lit candles. The altar was done perfect in purples and reds and blacks.

"You didn't need that fanfare but it added to the mystique." Rabouin continued:

> My biggest thing in schools and colleges when I was the ambassador for hell was you're well indoctrinated in the ancient, old, forbidden religion which might sound crazy to other people, but when you look at it, it's the closest thing to a Catholic service. When you think of how many times they used to introduce me, "Here's Ted Rabouin, the priest of witchcraft" and the awestruck audience would whisper, "This guy's crazy."
>
> I'd say, "Pretend you don't know who I am, but pretend you're following me at midnight and we're going to go to an old gothic looking place—the church. And there's a man, an educated man with a Ph.D. and every other thing, who's spent years in the seminary. He's going to be putting a dress on and he girds himself with a rope around his waist, and while he's doing it, he's talking to the clothes.
>
> "May this vestment make me pure. May these three cords of poverty, chastity, and obedience. May this chastible around my neck . . ." And he's starting to mumble to clothes, an educated man, and there you are, all thinking I'm crazy, and you wait as a man comes out and he kisses an altar stone . . .

Do you know what's in the stone? Bones of the saints. And he says to some bones, "May the bones of the saints whose relics lie herein I plead before the throne of God . . ." And he says it in an ancient language. (This was back when Latin was used.)

Then he incenses the altar, and he's all dressed in apostolic garb. After he kisses the altar, he goes up, he takes a piece of bread and he mumbles something. "Hoc est inum corpus meum." And it's no longer bread. It's God, Himself, who's present. Then you desecrate Him and eat Him . . . Cannibalistic act!

Then you drink his blood. . . .

How much more bizarre is my religion than yours? And then you say that spiritualism is holding seances? Why that man just asked the bones of the saints who they belong to to speak to God. Talking to dead people? Talking to dead people?

The blessed Mother, was she a woman or was she God?

She was a woman.

How long has she been dead? 2000 years and you're talking to her?

And then all of a sudden someone comes in with some salt in a round circled font, sprinkles some magic water, sprinkles some salt, and mumbles some ancient names of a deity, and all of a sudden the sin is washed away?

What about circumcision? What about when they desecrate a human being, cut off parts of his skin. If it was there for a reason? But no. Cut off somebody's skin? Yell and scream incantations.

Little black boxes where sins are forgiven and peaceful priests walking around in morbid clothes— black garb—for a God they proclaim is alive and well.

Doff the mourning clothes! Be happy if your God's alive and well. You all kill Him and you all eat Him and you all commit a cannibalistic act. Here's a man

with a Ph.D. genuflecting in front of a piece of bread.
It better be either Christ Himself because if it's just
bread then you're going to have to pay in eternity for
idolatry.

The talk Rabouin used was much longer, but the impact of
his early statements are obvious. He had a charisma, and the
cadence in his voice rivaled the best of the evangelical
preachers. He was not a hypnotist but a gifted speaker who
knew how to work his audience so that they were moved
emotionally without thinking logically.

Upon reflection, Rabouin was able to see some of the ways
in which he was seduced into the world he dominated for
many years. When he was young and troubled, he would go to
church, pray, and try to lead the life he felt he should. He
knew he had problems. He knew his sexual preference went
against the norms of society and the teachings of the Bible,
yet, he felt comfortable with God and thought he answered his
prayers sometimes.

"But then I became a spoiled brat," Rabouin explained. He
wanted instant gratification for all his desires. He prayed to
God at first, but nothing happened the way he wanted. Instead
of changing his immature attitude, he said to himself, "Well,
if God won't give it to me, the Devil will."

"The occult itself is so camouflaged in niceties that one
doesn't even realize when they're in it that they're in any form
of the tentacles, if you want to call it that, of Satanism. You go
in out of curiosity, and the curiosity turns into a reality, and
the reality gets a person in deeper. Then deeper they go, until
they find themselves in a maze they can't get out of.
Astrology—people are so saturated by it now—but that's an
avenue for Satanism. Palmistry, fortune telling, this Seth and
reincarnation. The Devil, I think, is in his heyday right now
and indeed he is loose for a little season and he's raking in as
much as he can. I find, myself, now that I have my own head
together, that the temptations now, as far as for me, are

astronomical. I've never had so many people ask me to cast a spell—'Oh, please, just one. They'll offer me thousands of dollars.'

"There's no avenue of the occult that I would say is safe."

Ted Rabouin was unusual in his pursuit and eventual leaving of Satanism in that he was not formally educated in the manner of so many individuals who pursue Satan. He was forced to leave school, taunted for his homosexuality, always told by his teachers that he would never amount to anything regardless of his intelligence. When he appeared with David Frost, Johnny Carson, and others, he felt vindicated. He had become someone. Taunts of childhood had come back to haunt the teachers and students who once had ridiculed him. He was important and had power, respect, and the key to a secret world that seemed capable of providing him and those who came to him with anything they wanted.

Although Rabouin is an exception, most Satanists are well-educated. The emotional reasons for abandoning Christ may be similar, but the leaders are neither fools nor crazies from a horror film. Michael Aquino's Ph.D., earned before he formed the Temple of Set, is not an unusual education background.

ACCEPTED IN THE BELOVED

Rabouin delighted in the manipulation of others. He understood why people sought the church, and he understood what took them from it. He spoke of people seeking guidance but being stopped by the church secretary with such lines about the priest as "he plays golf every Wednesday afternoon. He needs his rest, poor dear; he works so hard. I just make it a policy of not letting anything be scheduled that would interrupt his game. Let me schedule you for some other time, some other day."

Rabouin discovered through his observations that although the priests were hardworking, they seemed to be overprotective of their own time. He decided to make himself the equivalent of a convenience food store, opening his home to those seeking solace twenty-four hours a day. Whenever someone came or called, he or she was not turned away. "They asked for help and they went away filled. Whatever their need, whether it was to have someone listen to them or to request a spell, I satisfied them. They would complain about their ministers, their priests. I gave them what the clergy was not providing. And who do you think appeared to be the most spiritual? The churches were providing me with souls because they were not doing their job."

Although some Satanists are violent and perverted, most are not. The majority who have been interviewed are searching souls who feel themselves betrayed by the church as they know it. Sometimes they come from strict fundamentalist backgrounds where they have been taught that certain behavior is unforgivable such as wet dreams, unfulfilled sexual attractions, and a one-time "God damn." They do not sense forgiveness; they do not understand a God who saves not only from that which is truly sin but also from that which is simply unfounded guilt. They know only a God of vengeance who calls to heaven those without "spot or wrinkle."

Tragically, when people are exposed to this hybrid Christianity, a sense of hopelessness sets in. They are not aware that some pronouncements are both nonsense and unbiblical. They do not perceive that the "perfect" religious leaders are flawed and human, and that their teachings are contrary to Christ's words. Such blind teachers fail to see his love and acceptance for the repentant prostitutes, money changers, and tax collectors.

And if the religious seeker does not understand that failing humans can change, can grow, can embrace God's forgiveness, then a sense of hopelessness sets in. They feel rejected by God, yet they need to know and love a higher power. Instead of seeking another church, a place where compassion dominates instead of guilt, they presume that all Christianity is the same. If it is too late for heaven, why not obtain joy from the darker side, since hell is an inevitable destination for their souls based on what they have been taught?

Besides the religious seeker, the other type of person that turns to Satanism is the one that wants to worship a "magic" God. Most of the doctors, nurses, clergy, and other members of caretaking professions share this belief when they decide to worship Satan. They have always believed that there is a direct cause and effect between their actions and their rewards on earth. They can't understand a God who lets good people die in agony and innocent children suffer crippling injuries. They conclude that if there is a God, he certainly is not loving, so waiting for pleasure is senseless because pleasure will never come. Life is a sham. The reward of heaven is probably a myth, so why do right?

The lure of Satanism is that there is no wrong. We can have whatever pleasure we desire. We can pursue the man or woman of our choice. We can do whatever is necessary to obtain the hedonistic pleasures available to us all. There may be a time for suffering; but if that suffering is a natural part of life, why not obtain the joys that we have been told were wrong? We may lie, cheat, commit adultery, do whatever we desire, because in the end, nothing matters.

For a few, Satanism is an excuse to commit even the most vile of acts. Frequently these are not individuals who belong to organized satanic groups. These may be loners or people who travel in twos or threes, having discovered others with shared interest in violence just by chance.

The loners are the ones who seem to take the majority of the headlines. In Houston, Texas, five teenagers who said they were Devil worshipers were accused of torturing a man to death behind a cemetery in August of 1985. Two years earlier, three men were convicted of what a Chicago criminal court judge called crimes "shocking beyond human imagination." Black prostitutes were kidnapped and tortured, then their breasts were removed, placed on a Satanic altar, and eaten.

In October of 1985, Fuster Escalone, an ex-convict, was

convicted of sexual abuse in Miami, Florida. He sexually abused children during rituals where they prayed to Satan.

David Atwood, a devil worshiper serving time for burglary at the California Youth Authority, allegedly used magazine staples to carve *Satan* on his chest. He told a reporter from the San Francisco Examiner that he sometimes craves blood and welcomes death. He was quoted as saying, "Death frees me. It thrills me. It's no big deal."

The cases continue, as many as several hundred each year from all parts of the United States. Individuals who have decided to worship Satan, in whatever manner, go forth and commit crimes in the Devil's name. Sometimes they are found with *The Satanic Bible* in their possession, supposedly following its teachings. Other times they work out their own ways to practice Satanism, their approach based on fantasy, myth, movies, books, or whatever else their minds might decide. Kidnappings, rapes, murders, torture, and other violence are justified.

These loners are the most readily spotted as disturbed individuals. They are often psychotic, their language not necessarily coherent, their logic distorted. They may be wild-eyed, on drugs, unwashed, or otherwise unsavory. They are different, at times reclusive, at other times shunned as being "crazy." If they did not worship Satan, they would still be involved with violence and deadly antisocial behavior.

The reality of contemporary Satanism is that the majority of the people are "nice." They are our neighbors, our co-workers, perhaps our friends who lead a rather different private lifestyle. Their numbers are not great, but they exist in every community. And when they are with those of like minds, they will do things that they might otherwise never consider.

Ted Rabouin explained his approach. He would find a recruit, perhaps a doctor, lawyer, or clergyman, determine why he wanted to join a satanic group, then fulfill that need. If the aspiring member began to trust the power of Satanism through some apparent proof of Satan's "love," he would take the initiate into the group by having the person perform whatever obscene act Rabouin desired. The greater the humiliation he could inflict, the more certain he was of control. Such acts were not repeated in rituals but were used as Rabouin's test to see how dedicated the person would be. He had power, control, the respect he had always craved, and a growing list of souls for Satan.

DEVIL-DANCER: ANTON LAVEY

Two men must be considered among the most important in the field of contemporary American Satanism. One is Anton Szandor LaVey, who might be called the father of current satanic practices and beliefs. LaVey, the founder of the Church of Satan, wrote *The Satanic Bible*, a book that is owned by almost everyone interested in the occult. Many followers of *The Satanic Bible* hold allegiance to LaVey. In most instances he has neither heard of them nor heard from them. Yet these people commit crimes in his name, excuse passionate excesses in his name, and generally feel themselves to be a part of him. In the extreme, rapes, tortures, murder, and mutilation have been committed in the belief that he would approve. Yet his true influence is far less than the credit he is given and far more than his detractors would like.

The other man is Michael Aquino, the holder of a Ph.D. in political science, a college professor, and a career military reservist whose assignments frequently involve psychological operations. His assignments have taken him from the Presidio Military Base in the San Francisco area, his primary posting, to Washington, D.C., the NATO base in Germany, and elsewhere. He is founder of the Temple of Set, which was created in opposition to the perceived lowering of standards for membership in the Church of Satan. He is also a man whose primary followers are from the military, frequently members or former members of military intelligence.

Anton LaVey, especially, is the focal point for justifying many actions ranging from greed and lust to rape, torture, and murder, by individuals who have no connection with the Church of Satan. So many people have purchased *The Satanic Bible* as justification for their actions that LaVey is given credit for being involved with everything from white slavery to ritual human sacrifice.

One reason for the confusion is the way in which LaVey's writing gives the average person a reason for doing anything that he or she chooses. For example, *The Satanic Bible* describes magic as "the change in situations or events in accordance with one's will, which would, using normally accepted methods, be unchangeable." He then goes on to define the reality of humans engaging in any form of magic by saying:

> There is no difference between "White" and "Black" magic, except in the smug hypocrisy, guilt-ridden righteousness, and self-deceit of the "White" magician himself. In the classical religious tradition, "White" magic is performed for altruistic, benevolent, and "good" purposes; while "Black" magic is used for self-aggrandizement, personal power, and "evil" purposes. No one on earth ever pursued occult studies, metaphysics, yoga, or any other "white light" concept, without ego gratification and personal power as a goal.

In other words, no matter what one does, the motivation is consistent, one's actions are always accepted, no matter how good or how bad they may be.

For example, suppose an individual feels that God has failed because of the hunger, war, and other problems in the world. This person may invoke Satan's name in order to feed the starving, end violence, and otherwise improve the human condition. Such an individual is angry with God and determined to help end problems that should not exist. Although the approach may be questionable, the ends are considered to be good ones. The person might be classed as an eccentric, but everyone would applaud the causes he or she has taken to heart.

The problem comes with the opposite extreme, the individual who feels that he has been hurt and must seek revenge, personal pleasure, and other ends at the expense of others. In the extreme, this may mean murder, which, to a degree, is condoned by La Vey. For example, in his chapter entitled "On the Choice of Human Sacrifice," he says:

> Therefore, you have every right to (symbolically) destroy them, and if your curse provokes their actual annihilation, rejoice that you have been instrumental in ridding the world of a pest! If your success or happiness disturbs a person—you owe him *nothing!* He is made to be trampled under foot! *IF PEOPLE HAD TO TAKE THE CONSEQUENCES OF THEIR OWN ACTIONS, THEY WOULD THINK TWICE.*

Problems arise because of the disturbed thinking of those who have read such words. The kidnapping and rape of a woman can be justified in that she was giving pleasure to others and denying her aggressor. Damaging a car so it will crash can be justified because, if the person deserves to live, God will intervene. The list is endless, providing information that can justify any carnal, murderous, or greedy desire.

History, of course, is filled with Christians who have

misinterpreted the Bible. They have justified such acts as slavery, the suppression of women, and the denial of other human rights by either quoting the Bible out of context or simply creating Bible passages where none existed. Just as God cannot be held responsible for the reckless acts of Christians, it would be unfair to lay all satanic acts at the feet of Anton LaVey.

Michael Aquino's group claims to be more intellectual than LaVey's, having the strict standards for advancement that LaVey allegedly had lost. A large reading list is sent to members and those interested in the Temple of Set. It is also a reading list that has a number of books related to Hitler and his dreaded SS. Hitler had a strong interest in nontraditional religious beliefs, including various cults such as Satanism. This fact has led former members to charge that Aquino has a Nazi bias, is bigoted, and has followers who occasionally dress as Nazis.

Within the Temple, there is denial of extreme behavior. Aquino rightfully points out that there can be important aspects of a man's life and work, even if the man is personally reprehensible. It is thus possible to separate Hitler the scholar from Hitler the murderer.

Yet many of the followers allegedly are not so mature. They find the Nazi era and the study of Hitler very appealing, but this does not mean that they are encouraged at the top. It does not even mean that Aquino is aware of their actions. Again, in this regard, investigators are met with more questions than answers.

TALES OF GROWING UP

Born on 11 April 1930, Anton Szandor LaVey was raised in superstition and magic. His father was a traveling liquor salesman who, with his wife, wanted their son to be raised in a normal American manner. But by the time Anton was seven, he was reading books related to the occult. This fact so delighted his maternal grandmother, a woman born in Transylvania, that she began telling him the tales of her native land.

Transylvania was the land in which Dracula was said to have lived, and the folktales of the area were fascinating to a child. She told of such superstitions as the howling of dogs before someone died, as well as true stories of family members who had earned their living working the circus and carnival circuits. She did not try to influence his religious beliefs because the family was not actively involved with any religion. Thus as he grew older, the occult held the greatest fascination for him.

LaVey was somewhat of a loner in high school. He had little interest in sports and hated physical education classes. However, he did develop an interest in horror films he got to see when accompanying an uncle to Germany after the end of World War II. The uncle was a civilian engineer sent over to help repair air strips, and he was allowed to take Anton with him under a family visa.

One of the horror films allegedly told of a secret society of Satan worshipers, a concept that intrigued the growing teenager. He intensely studied the occult upon his return. The works ranged from volumes on black magic to stories about magicians themselves. He also read the work of Aleister Crowley, the founder of the Golden Dawn around the turn of the century. From Crowley had evolved the Church of Thelema, which had headquarters in Pasadena, California.

Other passions also consumed his time. Anton still had his high school studies to complete. He began studying judo during a period when the sport was not yet popular in the United States. He also took up the oboe after ten years of playing the violin. He was good enough so that when he turned sixteen, during his junior year in high school, he was able to leave the school and work as second oboist for the San Francisco Ballet Orchestra.

Playing with the orchestra was Anton's first introduction to show business, but his tastes manifested themselves in more flamboyant ways. In 1947 he obtained a job with the Clyde Beatty Circus, starting as a roustabout and cage boy who had to feed and water the lions. Later he convinced Beatty to let him learn to be an animal trainer.

Anton would later discuss this period with fondness. In a sense, he learned to adapt to a new society. He discovered that attitude was extremely important when working with lions because of their great physical size and strength. It was possible to be severely mauled in normal play because the human body is frail by comparison with that of the lion. What would be normal roughhousing among cubs and grown lions could destroy human flesh in moments.

LaVey grew close to the animals, spending much of his time with them so they would accept him. He also learned to create an image of danger for the lions when he was knocked over, an image that would prevent them from attacking until he could either stand or strike them with a stick to move them back.

Much has been made of the lion taming by both supporters and detractors of LaVey, but the truth seems to be that it was another adventure in his life. He was a man whose intellect was great and who constantly sought challenges. Once he had mastered lion taming, such a career proved boring. He decided to stay with the circus but to return to the music that he loved.

The calliope is the one circus instrument that denotes a carnival in its very sound. LaVey had taught himself to play the piano and wanted a chance to learn the calliope. This opportunity was almost denied to him, the regular player apparently being jealous of the young upstart. However, the regular player was also an alcoholic who was eventually fired by Beatty and replaced by LaVey at the last minute before a performance. It is not known how well Anton played that first night, but he was kept on at his position.

Playing the calliope was not a behind-the-scenes job. LaVey was a showman who had delighted in wearing black pants, a red silk shirt, a massive mustache, and long hair while working with the lions. He was equally outlandish as a calliope player, and so Beatty placed the instrument on a flatbed truck and Anton led the circus parade into each new town. There were also handbills declaring him to be:

Professor Anton Szandor LaVey

The Great Szandor

Player of the Calliope

Both Steam and Air

And Artist and Manipulator of the Aeolian Band Organ, Orchestmelochor, Apollonicon, Moscow Chimes, Oriental Music Car, Campbellican Pipes, Uni-Fon, and the Wurlitzer Unit Orchestra

Whose Music will brighten the hearts of children of all ages . . . And stir or soothe the most ferocious beasts of the jungle!

As ridiculous as the billing might be, LaVey did begin working to master a wide variety of musical instruments and techniques for playing. He was much like the early theater organists who played for the silent movies, varying the sounds according to the action on the screen. They would use the keyboard to create tension or a feeling of romance, announce the villain, and add to the sense of peril by the heroine. They gave silent movies an emotional impact they otherwise would have lacked.

LaVey learned to play the organ and other instruments in a similar manner. He would create tension for the performers who were risking their lives on the high wire and with other dangerous tricks. He would enhance the humor of the clowns, and generally adapt his playing to whatever the act. Once again he was a manipulative showman, a talent that would carry him well in the future.

LaVey was with Beatty only until the season ended in October of 1947. This was followed by jobs with Craft's

Twenty Big Shows and Pike Amusement Park in Long Beach, California.

Now the playing was different. This was a carnival with instruments such as the Wurlitzer and Hammond organs. The music would accompany everything from dancing girls to sideshow freaks. Some of the acts were questionably legal; others were scams, such as the fortune tellers and palm readers.

LaVey periodically worked the area with the scams. The tricks of fortune telling, palm reading, astrology, and other frauds used in the carnivals delighted him. He recognized that the public wanted to believe what they were seeing. The acts may have been frauds, but the crowd wanted to suspend disbelief and become a part of the act. They either delighted in being taken or pathetically believed in the "reality" of what they were seeing.

MARILYN MONROE

Perhaps one of the most talked about periods in LaVey's life was the time with Marilyn Monroe. This is a subject that her biographers often avoid or question, yet there is little doubt that LaVey and Monroe were together for a period of time.

In 1948 LaVey began playing the organ for burlesque shows. Comedy acts with sexual innuendos were a part of this as well as girls taking off their clothes. A good organ player could create different moods and enhance the popularity of the shows, so LaVey found himself working in the Burbank and the Mayan strip clubs.

Marilyn, then a bleached blonde, was on her way to success but by a rather long, slow path. She had been featured in a number of girly magazines and had been involved with two forgettable movies. Her first was the Twentieth Century Fox film *Dangerous Years*. The second, for which she had a more serious billing, was for Columbia's *Ladies of the Chorus*, in which she ironically played a stripper.

At Columbia she had a conflict with Harry Cohn, the studio

head. Cohn had an insatiable sexual appetite and delighted in making maximum use of the casting couch. Supposedly Cohn had identical offices with adjoining passageways that allowed him to "audition" a man on one side and a woman on the other, each thinking that they had been in "the" Cohn office. Whatever the truth about Cohn, sex with him seems to have been a sure way to advance a career.

Cohn did not bed every actress who passed through Columbia pictures. Many young stars refused him, and some were able to continue working for Columbia despite not yielding to his excesses. Others, such as Monroe, were not so fortunate. When Marilyn refused his advances, he chose to have her shunned within the industry. She was too new and too lacking in an audience for anyone to care at that time, so the young actress discovered no one wanted to hire her. She was staying alive by working the strip clubs.

Marilyn Monroe was a woman who gave the impression of having used her sexual appeal for her career, but she was always a vulnerable, childlike woman whose personal life totally lacked the flamboyance of her screen appearances. Performing as a striptease dancer was not a particularly comfortable role for her. She was awkward, following routine moves instead of playing off the audience as some of the women were able to do. For her, the type, quality, and beat of the music were all extremely important; thus the skills of LaVey improved her performance.

LaVey recognized Marilyn's vulnerability, and the two of them became friends. Soon they were lovers, each delighting in the closeness of a relationship during a period of high stress in their lives. Although Monroe worked enthusiastically as a stripper because she respected any work she did, she was hurting from the studio rejections of her acting. LaVey apparently was lonely at this time, so having a bedmate offered him comfort. Neither was looking for longterm commitment. Neither was likely to be able to relate to the other over time, their personalities and goals being quite different.

The one interest they both shared was magic. Marilyn was fascinated by the carny games and had Anton show her some of the tricks that were used. However, even this was not much of a bond, for after a few short, intense weeks, he became involved with another woman, one who was wealthy and could provide financial benefits to him. This relationship was also short, but it was enough to destroy the friendship with Marilyn that had been building.

ALL THINGS BY THE LAW

By winter of 1948, LaVey was on the move again. This time he traveled to San Francisco where he worked two jobs. He was an organ player for various stag affairs, continuing to support the strippers with his music. He also became a photographer for Paramount Photo Sales, a company that sold pictures of naked women.

The Korean War was starting in 1949, and LaVey realized that he was vulnerable to the draft. He decided to avoid war duty by attending college. He faked his lack of prior education and became a criminology student at the City College of San Francisco. He also worked as a piano player for fundraising events supporting various left-wing causes. However, his need for a greater income resulted in his working in burlesque houses the following year.

For a man as notorious in the minds of many as LaVey has become, the job he took in 1951 is both a shock and, to some, an embarrassment. Having married a banker's daughter, he took a job that was "straight." He became a photographer and assistant criminologist for the San Francisco Police Department.

LaVey's work may have been respectable, but it brought him into contact with the worst excesses of society—murders, arsons, fights, and numerous other situations where people were killed, maimed, or seriously injured. Frequently the horrors would be watched by passersby, few of whom became involved, even when their actions might have stopped some of the injury.

It was allegedly during this time that LaVey came to feel that perhaps there was no God. He was deeply bothered by a hit-and-run case in which a small girl was struck and killed by a car while the child's mother watched from the porch of their home. The girl was returning from her first day in school, a delightful time she apparently was going to share with her mother. The horror was so great that LaVey felt that God, as he understood Him, could not exist and allow such a tragedy.

The accident apparently triggered a philosophical change in LaVey. He recognized that frequently Satan was seen as the deity who walks among men, becoming involved with their affairs. It was Satan who seemed to take a direct interest in mankind and their earthly affairs. Perhaps Satan could supply a rational concept of life to explain what he had seen in his police work.

LaVey's involvement with the satanic began more as an observer than a participant. He attended services at a Berekely Church of Thelema, a group that was involved with occult study and philosophy. Then he read about the death of the leader and saw newspaper speculation as to the nature of the people. Stories indicated that the group was comprised of Satan worshipers who committed vile, dark, but unnamed deeds.

LaVey realized that the public was fascinated by Satanism to such a degree that almost any group of eccentrics could be accused of having orgies. He managed to persuade the police to let him investigate what were passed off as "nut" cases—such as unexplained phenomena reported as ghosts. Some of the regular officers saw the investigation of such matters as a waste of time; others feared involvement with the supernatural.

THE MAGIC MAN

In 1955 Anton LaVey quit the San Francisco Police Department to work in magic. Since this was a period of emotional excess in the United States, with the fear of Russians, the intolerance of others, the fascination with the Ouija Board, and the concept of past lives, the general public was seeking magic as an answer to their problems and their curiosity about life. They wanted someone greater than themselves, one who could guide them through the mysteries of life, since God couldn't seem to do it.

Of course, the problem was not God but weak individuals who were unwilling to take responsibility for their own lives. They were unable to handle the idea of free will and a life without "magic" answers. It was a period when a man like LaVey, a born showman who had practiced his skills in many ways, could set himself up in a leadership role and be accepted.

One of the first stages in becoming a leader was for Anton to change his appearance and develop a lifestyle quite different from his neighbors. Upon leaving the police department, he regrew his mustache, added a beard, and began wearing a long, black overcoat. He also obtained a black leopard as a pet, an animal that lived in the family apartment and accompanied LaVey on late night walks.

Walking the animal after dark was actually a kindness to the neighbors, since the tame animal would not be seen by so many people. However, when the man and his leopard were spotted, the darkness, the fog of San Francisco, and the harsh glow of the streetlights would combine to create a sinister, horror movie image quite different from reality.

Eventually LaVey moved into the former home of Mammy Pleasant. Mammy Pleasant, whose real name was Mary Ellen, was a woman whose reputation during the late nineteenth century was a notorious one. She was a highly successful businesswoman who was the subject of a scandalous trial after there were complaints about her from the wife of one of her clients. However, the greatest scandal of all came from the fact that Mammy Pleasant's money came, in part, from running a house of prostitution. It was alleged that she also practiced voodoo and black magic, but a check of historic records indicates no proof. It is certain that she was wealthy, a shrewd businesswoman, and one of the best madams in San Francisco.

The house itself had a disreputable flavor. Secret passages had been constructed in it to allow freedom of movement that would be unseen by the men. A customer could be robbed by a house employee without ever seeing the person who rifled his pants while he was being entertained by one of the prostitutes.

The house was quickly painted black, establishing LaVey as the community eccentric. However, Anton did not take full advantage of the house and the image it provided. He became an organist for both a nightclub and the city of San Francisco's conventions. He also became infatuated with a young woman named Diane, who worked as an usher at the Seaview Theater in Pacifica, California. Eventually he divorced his wife, married Diane, and in 1960 began holding weekly magic seminars.

The seminars might be considered the start of LaVey's notoriety. They were held at midnight on Friday, a delightfully theatrical touch, and included information on the occult and supernatural. For $2.50 a person, attendees would learn about subjects ranging from extrasensory perception (ESP) to voodoo. There was even a story, whether true or not, that a seminar on cannibalism was accompanied by a meal that supposedly included the cooked thigh of a white American female. Allegedly the thigh was provided by a physician from a biopsy of a woman after her death. Whatever the meat might have been, it was garnished with such items as yams and fried bananas, the traditional accompaniment for human flesh eaten by Figi islanders. It was probably nothing more sinister

81

than carefully prepared leg of lamb combined with a story some of his diners might have chosen to take as truth.

The story of the cannibalism again added to the ongoing mystery of Anton LaVey. Because of his showmanship, he could get away with acts that would be too outrageous for the average person to consider, yet his beliefs and the degree to which he would go as a Satanist are unknown. Thus, almost any story about the man, including a tale of cannibalism, white slavery, or murder, could be true. Certainly, if he denied it, he would do so in such a way as to leave the questioner uncertain of reality. Without actual proof, the questioner either damned LaVey as a man without a conscience or praised him as a man of vision.

The magic sessions began attracting a wide range of individuals, including physicians, actors, film producers, and others. LaVey had learned hypnosis as part of his interests and had patients referred to him for problems where hypnotherapy could be of value. The doctors who were part of his gatherings utilized his skills for weight problems, insomnia, and similar difficulties that could be treated through hypnosis.

In 1964 the combination of LaVey's library on the occult and a growing group of acquaintances and friends who were familiar with various rituals, made him one of the leading experts in the field. Reporters began to interview him, and he furthered his image by having a black cape with scarlet lining made for himself. Often it was worn with a top hat and sword cane.

Herb Caen, one of the most popular columnists in San Francisco, delighted in writing about LaVey, a fact that added to his notoriety. He discussed the pet leopard, LaVey's tarantula, and the lion named Togare, a gift from another former Clyde Beatty Circus trainer. When the lion was housebroken, much like a cat, the information delighted reporters; stories were run about LaVey's teaching the lion to fetch a doll and to come and eat whenever "Onward Christian Soldiers" was played on the piano.

THE CHURCH OF SATAN

It was on the night of 30 April 1966 that Anton LaVey's interest in the occult and the activities of what had once been known as his "Magic Circle" changed dramatically. To some, the change was a sinister foretelling of the Devil's return to earth. For others, it was the logical progression of a brilliant man who dared to explore areas of life many people felt were taboo. Anton LaVey started the Church of Satan.

The idea for the church apparently came from the suggestion of a police inspector friend. The man mentioned that LaVey's knowledge and philosophy could be the basis for a new religion.

The concept apparently intrigued LaVey right from the start. He recognized that his spells and rituals seemed to be of some benefit in changing circumstances in his life. He looked upon Christ as someone who might be considered a magician because of his actions. And the rituals of groups such as the Catholic Church all seemed to involve magic based on a fear of God. Why not start his own church?

The night of 30 April (Walpurgis Night) was traditionally a time for pagan festivals involving demons, witches, and orgies, so it seemed to fit with LaVey's usual showmanship. He shaved his head and declared the date to be I Anno Satanas, the first year after Satan regained earth. Even men who would become, in part, LaVey's critics and detractors within their own groups, such as Michael Aquino, date their activities from the same base.

The first year was a problem for LaVey. He was serious about Satanism as a philosophy and way of life. He was also continuing to present the various lectures and related activities within the community. Thus the image was that of a charlatan, a clown, a man who was dubbed The Black Pope by the press. Yet privately LaVey was reported to have said:

If they presume the Pope represents the Lord, I suppose it's all right for me to be thought of as the personification of Satan. Just be sure you understand that I have begun the Church of Satan as a true vehicle of the black arts. The other groups or covens have all represented white witchcraft, basing their use of magic on altruistic purposes. To be a true Satanist, doing something merely for altruistic reasons is senseless. Black magic is for personal power.

There were other problems as well, though many were unknown to LaVey. The publicity had a great influence on individuals who were interested in the occult. In Southern California, for example, police reported a number of groups committing crimes in the name of LaVey and the Church of Satan. Child abuse, ritual torture, and other actions were done to please LaVey, who knew nothing about such groups. He had become the focus for their psychopathic fantasies. They would carry out his messages, ones he never sent.

One such group in Southern California, as mentioned earlier, would eventually take credit for the death of Jayne Mansfield, the actress who became a Satanist during I Anno Satanas. The reasoning behind their actions was logical, but the truth remains a mystery because of the nature of her death.

JAYNE MANSFIELD

Jayne Mansfield was an actress with greater physical attributes than proven talents. She had blond hair and a magnificent bust line. She was a studio-hyped star who, along with Marilyn Monroe, was seen more as a sexy bimbo. Whether or not she had talent as an actress, as Monroe proved herself to have, would not be known because of the suddenness of her death.

Mansfield was never able to sustain a relationship. Her first husband was Mickey Hargitay, a man who won the Mr. Universe title. Early photographs of them looked much like contemporary illustrations for articles on health and fitness. Their bodies made them seem the perfect couple, two magnificent specimens totally in love with one another. Yet the relationship did not last.

Mansfield's second husband was Matt Climber, a film producer and businessman who was born Thomas Vitale Ottaviano. Again there was a divorce, this one more painful than the previous, with the press frequently writing about her child custody battle and other problems.

There was no third marriage, but Jayne became seriously involved with Sam Brody, her lawyer, lover, and manager. Brody was also an insecure, jealous man who was married at the time of his affair with Jayne. Oddly, Brody was considerably shorter than she was, older, and far less physically attractive than her ex-husbands. However, he offered Jayne a sense of security and what she felt was an intellectual attraction.

Allegedly Brody was Jayne's blackmailer as well as her lover. She was notorious for having affairs with any man she found physically attractive. Some of these proved to be setups by Brody who allegedly had her photographed during sex.

Jayne arranged to meet LaVey in 1966, became infatuated with him and his church, and was interested in joining. She also discussed with Lavey her child custody case, and he responded by offering counseling and allegedly putting a curse on Climber. Whether or not the latter is true, Climber did lose the child custody case to Mansfield.

Jayne began flaunting her involvement with the Church of Satan, much to Brody's disgust. She liked to be photographed in her robes, and she wore a Baphomet medallion LaVey had selected for members of the church. Brody hated the medallion, frequently tearing it from her neck when they would have fights. He was especially angry when she wore it to the San Francisco Film Festival in the fall of 1966. The medallion was quite noticeable with her extremely low-cut evening gown, a fact not lost on the television commentator interviewing the celebrities.

The day after the festival, Brody, Mansfield, and Mansfield's road manager stopped by LaVey's home. Brody began wandering through the house, mocking the various items he saw. He also lit a candle used for destruction rituals, an action that made LaVey irate when he discovered what had happened.

The film festival continued for a second evening, but this time Mansfield was not allowed to attend. She had chosen a gown so daring that a portion of her breasts was showing. Although the gown would have raised surprise at any time, twenty years after, other actresses would be at least as daring in order to gain attention at film festivals. However, at the time, such an action was shocking and not permitted. Jayne undoubtedly realized this when expelled, but she blamed Brody, claiming that his actions at the LaVey home had brought about her problems.

Jayne's growing infatuation with the Church of Satan was fueled by an incident in which Zoltan, her son by Mickey Hargitay, was mauled by a lion at Jungleland, a private zoo in Thousand Oaks. Jungleland was an area where wild animals were boarded and trained for show business appearances. The visitors were protected from the animals, but some, such as the lion, were only on chains. Zoltan wandered too close and was attacked by the big cat.

Just how serious the wounds might have been is not known. Zoltan's skull was fractured, his spleen was ruptured, and there were bone splinters at the base of the brain. He had to have emergency surgery; his survival chances were uncertain.

Jayne Mansfield turned to LaVey as her spiritual adviser and friend. She asked him for help, and he eventually performed two rituals, one related to the surgery and the other for complications from infection. Whether from magic, medical skill, or both, Zoltan recovered.

Jayne Mansfield fit nicely into this situation. She delighted in such actions as wearing extremely short skirts while not wearing panties. Then, when she stepped from a car or took some other position where her skirt was certain to ride up, she would announce that nobody should look, a statement made to ensure as many men staring as possible. She would deliberately weaken the fabric of some of her clothing, so that it would tear in strategically "embarrassing" areas, and do other things to call attention to her sexual areas.

LaVey so enjoyed Mansfield that he made her a priestess within the church, a charge she took seriously. Instead of continuing with the sexual games and stunts, she began studying the field of witchcraft and magic. She also had private rituals arranged for her, since she did not attend Friday night services.

Brody was becoming irate with LaVey. Jayne was calling LaVey daily, her relationship part friendship, part student, and part sexual fantasy, a fact that made Brody extremely jealous. Finally, in January of 1967, the anger resulted in Brody ordering LaVey to never talk with Jayne again. He called LaVey a charlatan and threatened to make trouble if the relationship did not stop.

LaVey, extremely angry, pronounced Sam Brody dead within one year. He then performed a destruction ritual guaranteed to destroy Brody's life. He also alerted Jayne to what he had done, a revelation that did not seem to upset her.

Mansfield wanted the relationship between Brody and LaVey to be reconciled. As much as she hated the oppressive jealousy of Brody, apparently she liked him enough that she was not ready to give him up. She also did not take LaVey's action as irreversible, and eventually she got Brody to apologize.

With Brody and LaVey at peace during February of 1967, Mansfield went to Vietnam to help entertain the troops, a fact that gave everyone some distance. LaVey had explained that the destruction ritual could not be reversed, but Jayne apparently did not fully comprehend what that could mean. She seemed happy, though her mood changed after her return when fights with Brody went from screaming matches to physical violence. According to Mansfield, Brody began beating her.

Word of the destruction ritual allegedly reached Alan Cambridge's group of Satanists living in Southern California. He later spoke of feeling compelled to carry forth the "orders" of Satan given through the form of Anton LaVey. He decided he would arrange for Sam Brody's death, or so he would say afterwards.

The destruction ritual performed by LaVey is unknown, though it can be presumed to be identical with the one he discussed in *The Satanic Bible*. He also explained human sacrifice, saying, in part:

> The use of a human sacrifice in a Satanic ritual does not imply that the sacrifice is slaughtered "to appease the gods." Symbolically, the victim is destroyed through the working of a hex or curse, which in turn leads to the physical, mental or emotional destruction of the "sacrifice" in ways and means not attributable to the magician.

At the end of the chapter, LaVey justified his earlier comment by saying:

> Mad dogs are destroyed, and they need far more help than the human who conveniently froths at the mouth when irrational behavior is in order! It is easy to say, "So what!—these people are insecure so they can't hurt me." But the fact remains—given the opportunity, they would destroy you.
>
> Therefore, you have every right to [symbolically] destroy them, and if your curse provokes their actual annihilation, rejoice that you have been instrumental in ridding the world of a pest! If your success or happiness disturbs a person—you owe him nothing! He is made to be trampled under foot! IF PEOPLE HAD TO TAKE THE CONSEQUENCES FOR THEIR OWN ACTIONS, THEY WOULD THINK TWICE!

What does this mean! Anything a believer desires. If something evil happens to the individual so cursed, then the curser can take full credit. On the other hand, if it does not work, then whatever misfortunes befall the cursed probably are considered punishment enough. Real or not, such a curse by the leader of the Church of Satan would have tremendous impact on the followers. If Jayne Mansfield was actually murdered, the people who committed the crime were not connected with LaVey except in their psychopathic fantasies. Yet all credit would go to LaVey's curse, an action he would not deny and one the actual killers would defend as instruments of a "leader" whom they had never met.

Jayne Mansfield remained involved with Sam Brody after LaVey warned her not to be near him. On 28 June 1967, a young man named Ronnie Harrison drove Jayne, Brody, and Mansfield's three children by first husband Mickey Hargitay to New Orleans. Jayne had been appearing in Biloxi, Mississippi, at the Gus Stevens Restaurant and Supper Club but was scheduled to be on television the following morning.

It was foggy on U.S. 90 and Harrison was driving fast, his speed estimated to be at least eighty miles per hour. He was believed to have been drinking as well.

The car hit the rear end of a tank truck that was spraying for mosquitoes, killing the three adults and nearly decapitating Jayne. The children were injured but recovered.

According to Heather Cambridge, daughter of Alan Cambridge who allegedly set up Mansfield, the Los Angeles Satanists felt that it was their job to fulfill the curse on Brody. They were in New Orleans at the time and allegedly went to where Jayne had been playing; then they made a pinhole puncture in the brake line. It would only be after the car was driven that the brakes would fail from fluid leakage, and then it would be too late to correct the problem.

What really happened is unknown, but basically, the car did not stop. There were no skid marks, no indication that the driver tried to brake.

The situation at the scene indicates two possibilities. One is that the car could not stop, a scenario that would have the young driver frantically working his brakes as the truck loomed into view. He would only have seconds, not enough time to realize what was happening and try to steer around the truck.

On the other hand, the driver could have been too tired to think clearly and react swiftly. There was fog on the road; it was early morning; and the driver had been drinking. By the time the sight of the truck registered in his mind, his reactions may have been too slow to make stopping possible. If this happened, there also would have been no skidmarks, the brakes never having been applied.

Jayne Mansfield's death enhanced the reputation of Anton LaVey among some of his followers. He had performed the destruction ritual against Brody and he was dead. Jayne had not heeded the warning to stay away from the man, so she died, too, though her death was most upsetting for LaVey. It was an unusual incident in an unusual life.

THE OFFICIAL WORD

In 1967 another important change came for the Church of Satan—acceptance as a religion. This occurred in December when Edward Olsen, a member of the church and a seaman in the U.S. Navy, died. He requested that he receive a satanic funeral, a request that LaVey fulfilled. A full Navy honor guard was also present, a fact that was tacit approval of Satanism by the military. Although this may or may not have been a deliberate statement on the part of the Navy, what happened was extremely controversial.

The ceremony itself was rather low key. The eulogy included the statement:

We are not here today to consign Edward Olsen to the heavenly realm. He would not have wanted that. He believed that the concept of Heaven and Hell lies within the framework of our minds and our bodies, and he found them to be one and the same. He chose the path of Satan because he believed the living flesh that created and gave birth to him, his father and mother, were much more marvelous and real than any God he could not see. He believed that his good, true friends were more important than any unknown saints. If this be blasphemous, then why not walk the Devil's path? The Earth needs more people like Edward Olsen.

Today Satanism is accepted by military policy that prevents religious discrimination. However, despite the fact, the reactions among the chaplains are interesting. When we contacted the chaplains at the Presidio, where Lt. Col. Michael Aquino, the head of the Temple of Set, was based, one chaplain made disparaging remarks about the policy. He was against any form of Satanism as an accepted religion. At the same time, he understood the policy and told how they have to put up with it, though he would prefer that such a group only be active off the base.

A second chaplain said that he had heard of Aquino, but he did not know him personally and accepted the fact that this was a religion there because the law allowed it. A third chaplain informed us that he had neither heard of the Temple of Set nor had he ever heard of Michael Aquino. Then he corrected the pronunciation of Aquino's last name.

It was not until 1969 that the Church of Satan went national from its San Francisco base. LaVey charged thirteen dollars to anyone interested in joining. For their money they received a questionnaire designed to determine their interest and reasons for wanting to join, a number of essays on Satanism, and, eventually, information on the performance of a basic ritual, the latter supplied only if the person was found to be acceptable.

LaVey was also refining his psychological understanding of how the average person is affected by Satanism. He realized that it is possible to plant ideas into someone's mind. For example, if he sprinkled a supposedly magic powder on the floor and said that any person who stepped on it would make mistakes all day, somebody might believe what he had said. Such a person might become careless, seemingly making "magic" work. Some spells might work because of the powers of Satanism, but others might work because, knowing what has been done, the person makes it self-fulfilling.

LaVey was also riding the crest of popular interest in Satanism. Author Ira Levin had written a successful novel entitled *Rosemary's Baby* that told the story of an actor who sold his soul to the devil and turned his firstborn child over to Satan. Rosemary, his wife, is impregnated during a ritual that brings Satan to earth to be the father of the child. Thus her baby is the Devil's child.

The book was extremely popular and made into a movie in 1967. Between the time when the book was optioned and the filming begun, a story appeared in the news about Anton LaVey's daughter, Zeena, who was baptized into Satanism by her father. The child allegedly was unusual, including having the ability to walk by electrical appliances and have them suddenly short circuit without any logical explanation for the happenings.

In addition, Zeena supposedly was unusually articulate when pronouncing satanic names. She also played with her father's pet lion without difficulty or fear. She seemed to be so much her father's child that the baptism was a logical action. It also tweaked the noses of leaders of organized religions and thus made good copy for the newspapers. Levin read about the situation, and LaVey was hired to work a couple of weeks with the movie company.

The film itself was entertainment. Although some of the satanic practices shown were close to reality, most had nothing to do with the church's rituals.

THE SATANIC BIBLE

The most important work LaVey performed in order to bring Satanism to America came in 1968 when he developed his philosophy into a book called *The Satanic Bible*. The book, which appeared two years later as an Avon paperback, was divided into two sections. The first relates the philosophy and reasoning of Satanism. The second details the practice of satanic magic. Overall, it is an attack on what is often called the Judeo-Christian ethic. It is also extremely self-centered, a volume meant to justify personal indulgence even at the expense of others. The general idea is that no one owes anything to anyone.

There would be other works, including *The Compleat Witch, Or What To Do When Virtue Fails,* but none would have the impact of *The Satanic Bible.* Suddenly there was a book that justified almost any excess or indulgence someone might wish to make. No matter what might have been intended, it was possible to read justification for it in the text.

Individuals who were highly disturbed frequently read *The Satanic Bible.* Murderers and rapists were, at times, found to have the book in their homes, leading to newspaper speculation that they were part of some widespread cult. In reality they were often fascinated by the book because they had a source for justifying their psychopathic desires and behavior. They were not led astray by the book; their crimes would have been committed whether it existed or not. But the book seemed to help them justify their feelings, making it easier for them to deal with their antisocial desires.

There was a second important factor with the book. It created a sense of personal acceptance for people. If a man was a transvestite, a homosexual, or a sexual abuser, he received there no condemnation from the Satanic Church. Whether or not LaVey or the members were comfortable with the person's desires, they accepted them as natural for the individual. LaVey simply played off the reality that many Christians do not share Christ's total love for humanity. They are intolerant and judgmental, neither of which fits biblical teaching, but they also represent the only aspect of the church some people will ever know. By comparison with these people, Satanism seems a logical choice.

DEVIL-ADVOCATE: MICHAEL AQUINO

For Michael Aquino, the second major figure in contemporary Satanism, if only by virtue of his military involvement, awareness of Anton LaVey came in 1968. Aquino was a University of California graduate and a recently commissioned army lieutenant. While attending the movie *Rosemary's Baby* in a San Francisco theater before leaving for his first assignment in North Carolina, he saw Anton LaVey for the first time. He learned of LaVey's church and, curious, decided to go to one of LaVey's lectures.

Aquino liked what he found in LaVey; both the intellectual aspects and the showmanship delighted him.

Michael Aquino is a brilliant man, the son of the late Betty Ford, a woman who was considered a child prodigy. Betty Ford also had a strong interest in the unusual; San Francisco area newspaper clippings indicate that she visited Germany in 1939 to study. Her interests may have been a factor in leading her son to the occult Nazi activities that continue to fascinate him.

Aquino's parents were divorced, and LaVey's wives had only daughter's, so the relationship that developed between them, at least on the part of Aquino, seemed close to being one of father to son or teacher to student.

This relationship led to rather unusual circumstances. In June of 1969, Aquino was sent to South Vietnam for a tour of duty. By the first part of 1970, he was director of psychological warfare teams acting as a support for the First Infantry Division. His base was Lai Khe, an area that was filled with housing that often ranged from bombed-out buildings to tents. Because the area was under periodic bombardment, the work was difficult.

THE "DIABOLICON"

As a personal exercise, Aquino decided to write what he calls a "restatement of certain themes from *Paradise Lost.*" Although this type of exercise, and others such as his later writing of a variation of the Indiana Jones story, was not unusual for the prolific Aquino, what evolved is extremely important. It was called "The Diabolicon," and it is a series of statements from Satan Archdaimon, Beelzebub, Azazel, Abaddon, Asmodeus, Astaroth, Belial, and Leviathan. Beelzebub is actually better known as Baal-zebub, a Philistine god ("lord of the flies") who was worshiped at Ekron. He was considered to be the controller of the flies and the prince of the devils. At one point it was believed that Jesus cast out devils through the power of Beelzebub (Luke 11:19), a belief based on the Jews' thinking of that time that heathen deities were demons.

Azazel was an evil spirit living in the Wilderness of Judea who was interconnected with ridding Israel of sin. A randomly selected goat was tossed over a cliff as a symbol of this ridding; this was connected with Azazel, who was at times mentioned as a scapegoat.

Abaddon was also known as Apollyon. He was the destroyer, the angel of the abyss (Rev. 9:11). And the others are also demons and evil creatures of one form or another, including Leviathan who is a sea creature or monster.

"The Diabolicon" is either allegory or direct message to mankind through Aquino, depending upon the reader's interpretation. Aquino himself later said,

> As I wrote the various passages, I seemed to sense precisely what they should say. And, if I penned words or phrases that "didn't fit," I would experience intolerable irritation and impatience until I had replaced them with the "correct" combination. It was as though the manuscript had a life of its own, and even when it was done I found myself unable to type it as I had originally intended to do. Instead I took another month to copy it into a finished book of two volumes in an odd calligraphic script that, once more, "imposed itself" on the project.

The various sections of "The Diabolicon" are not so important as the overall attitude toward religion that is shown within. For example, at the conclusion of the section entitled "The Statement of Satan Archdaimon" he wrote:

> I who am Lucifer, and who have taken the name of Satan Archdaimon, do bear this title with pride, for I am in truth the great enemy of all that is God. Together, man, thou and I shall achieve our eternal glory in the fulfillment of our will.

"The Diabolicon" was sent to LaVey in March of that year, and Aquino became a part of the satanic priesthood in June. He was also declared a member of the Council of Nine or Council of the Trapezoid, LaVey's governing body for the church. Although the members were theoretically the highest authorities within the church, in reality their powers and actions would vary as LaVey deemed necessary.

BONDING AND BREAKING

The two men began developing a relationship of mutual respect. How LaVey viewed his eager follower is unknown, but Aquino seemed to view LaVey as a cross between a father figure and a beloved teacher. He also delighted in some of his more theatrical activities.

In 1971, LaVey received new publicity for a book entitled *The Compleat Witch*. This was seemingly a radical departure for the man, since it was not a volume of potions and spells. Instead it was a manhunter's guide for women, almost a soft-core pornography version of books relating to ways to captivate a man.

LaVey's contention was that the attraction of the opposite sex is essentially an animal act. Society created all manner of rules and regulations, matters of etiquette, and similar restraints on the mating game. Yet the reality, according to LaVey, is that if a woman wants a man, she has to follow the animal within her.

The book went against the romantic notions of courtship. Women evidently did not appreciate his insights because the book did not succeed. Both the hardback and the paperback had brief runs in the bookstores before going out of print, despite numerous radio and television appearances by LaVey. However, the tour did keep LaVey before the public eye.

Church membership grew rapidly enough that LaVey began regional centers for the members. He utilized lay Satanists who acted as contact points for those members who were outside the specific Grottos, as the original centers were called, in Louisville, Dayton, Denver, and Detroit. This approach would let individuals in New York, Texas, and elsewhere feel more connected to an actual organization. It was an effective idea that also made the church more like a religious institution.

The actual structure also became more rigid. By 1970 there was a hierarchy that sounded a little like a formal church. For example, there was Apprentice I degree, Witch or Warlock II degree (a witch was always female, a warlock always male), the Priest or Priestess of Mendes III degree, Magister Caverni/Templi/Magus IV Degree, and Magus V degree. Special colors and medallions identified the different ranks. These were deliberately created to relate to the areas of Cardinal, Bishop, and Archbishop at the fourth degree level, with Magus V degree being the equivalent of the Pope. Obviously LaVey held that highest degree.

Communication among the members increased. A newsletter, "From the Devil's Notebook," was begun; the name soon changed to "The Cloven Hoof." The editing of this publication eventually was taken over by Aquino, who later would comment about how he added his own personal touch. He stated:

> Under my Editorship the newsletter got into all sorts of topics which the Church of Satan had not previously discussed to any great degree: the Great Pyramid of Giza, Nazi occultism, the creation of the Universe according to the theories of plasma physics matter/antimatter, prehuman and human evolution, archaeological developments bearing upon Satanism, life extension & life-after death, the actual existence of Satan as an intelligent entity, social forecasting, international economics & finance, etc.

These would be among the topics that continued to interest Aquino after he broke with the Church of Satan to form his own Temple of Set.

The growth of the Church of Satan was rapid but nowhere near the press notices of the 1970s. Estimates never denied by the church ranged from ten to twenty-five thousand members nationwide. Because many of those who bought *The Satanic Bible* like to think of themselves as members of the church, even though they never joined nor read its literature, it was easy for reporters anywhere in the country to find a LaVey

Satanist to quote. Yet the membership was only 250 to 300 people during this period. It was a small group with excellent public relations and a philosophy so out of step with society that it always made good copy on slow news days.

All was not well in hell, however. Anton LaVey was acting in a manner that was increasingly at odds with the standards for the church in which Michael Aquino believed. LaVey was periodically promoting someone to priesthood level without the person going through all the formal rites that had been expected of them. Leadership increasingly could be honorary and, it was suspected, purchased. To some member-critics, Satanism was running the risk of becoming little more than a diploma mill.

"NINTH SOLSTICE MESSAGE"

It was in the ninth year of the Church of Satan that the last intense goodwill seemed to exist between Aquino and LaVey. In the months to come, there would be increasing disagreements about a number of major issues related to the running of the church. But at this time the men were close, and again, Aquino took pen in hand for a Diabolicon-like message. Eventually called the "Ninth Solstice Message," it seemed to be written by Satan through the hand of Aquino. Whether Aquino believed this was a direct message or just a way of honoring LaVey is uncertain. However, the honor with which he held LaVey is obvious in the lines:

> By my Will, Anton Szandor LaVey, you are divest of your human substance and become in your Self a Daimon.
>
> Henceforth you are as a true god, and it is in your power to alter the machinery of the cosmos according to your desire. No charge do I lay upon you, for you are now my brother and no longer my liege. But remember always the word we of Hell have proclaimed. We need justify neither our existence nor our desires, but without a considered purpose—

which Belial has set forth in the Diabolicon—both are without consequence.

The text later quotes Satan as saying:

My Age has begun, and I am come forth to uphold my bond with mankind. Yet I shall not illuminate all, nor even many—but a few. I seek the Elect, who in turn seek me. Man the god shall arise only from the ashes of man the beast—The blood is the life.

It is interesting to look ahead a few years after this writing. If Michael Aquino was a tool of Satan in the manner of someone who does automatic writing triggered by an unknown force, then the Devil makes mistakes. If, on the other hand, this approach to writing is Aquino's way of establishing his own dogma in a religious style, then he wreaked vengeance in the same manner a few years later. Whichever was the case, after the break with LaVey, a new document was born.

"BOOK OF COMING FORTH BY NIGHT"

On the night of 21–22 June 1975, Michael Aquino wrote the "Book of Coming Forth by Night." He said:

My evocation—an effort to interpret the surprising downfall of the Church of Satan—was addressed to "Satan" (which I believed the proper name of the Prince of Darkness). Immediately, however, he reveals himself as Set. . . . As a god of darkness and the night, Set was the complement to Hor (god of the daylight) in predynastic times. So integral was this relationship that the heads of the two gods were frequently shown on a single body (hieroglyphic name: God of Two Faces).

In the writing of this book, the statements previously made to LaVey, especially his elevation to god status and equal of Satan, is suddenly changed. Apparently the Devil, Satan, Set, or whomever is a rather fickle god in his attitudes and beliefs, at least after Aquino makes his break. The reigning that LaVey should have had was taken from him as Set, through Aquino, stated, in part:

> Now it has come to pass, and the Book of the Law is laid bare—"Destined First Century heir—Aquino—breaking Keys by doctrines Anton LaVey—great Magus of reconsecration coming Year xeper—founding his rightful Priesthood—Set—true origin Volume AL" Michael Aquino, you are become Magus V degree of the Aeon of Set.

The contrast is striking. Did LaVey truly fall so far as to gain Set's anger in the previous year, or did Aquino lose an internal power struggle and, in the manner of a child with the only football on the block, get mad and take his god and go home? Set explained that he tolerated the era named for Satan:

> But this is now my Aeon, and my pentagram is again to be pure in its splendor. Cast aside the corruptions, that the pentagram of Set may shine forth. Let all who seek me never be without it, openly and with pride, for by it I shall know them.

Set explains that those who follow him, including Aquino, shall be known as Setians. The relationship is also far more personal than Satan apparently allowed:

> The Satanist thought to approach Satan through ritual. Now let the Setian shun all recitation, for the text of another is an affront to the Self. Speak rather to me as to a friend, gently and without fear, and I shall hear as a friend. Do not bend your knee nor drop your eye, for such things were not done in my house at PaMat-et. But speak to me at night, for the sky then becomes an entrance and not a barrier. And those who call me the Prince of Darkness do me no dishonor.

LaVey is dismissed sadly but logically in the hierarchy of the darker universe, the writing indicating that Aquino was always in line for greater glory. It was written:

> Upon the ninth Solstice, therefore, I destroyed my pact with Anton Szandor LaVey, and I raised him to the Will of a Daimon, unbounded by the material dimensions. And so I thought to honor him beyond other men. But it may have been this act of mine that ordained his fall.
>
> Were I my Self to displace the Cosmic Inertia, I should be forced to become a new measure of consistency. I would cease to be One, for I should become All.
>
> To make of a man a Daimon, then, may be to break his Self-reference to the bounds in which his semblance must exist.

Looking at this revelation logically is a rather interesting exercise. Nothing in LaVey's life or the life of the Satanist followers seemed to indicate dramatic changes in 1974. LaVey did not become Superman. LaVey did not seem to develop cosmic awareness and insight into the universe that made him any more formidable, or vulnerable, than in the past. The masses did not rise up to acknowledge his leadership and the dark world did not dominate the land.

In addition, why were the events not predictable? If Set was so powerful, why did he not realize what would happen? More importantly, after reading the next quote, one wonders why LaVey was elevated at all if Aquino was the favored one as it implies.

> In the fifth year of the Church of Satan, I gave to this Magus my Diabolicon, that he might know the truth of my ancient Gift to mankind, clothed though it might be in the myths of the Hebrews. Even you, who delivered the Diabolicon from Asia, did not know it for what it was. But he that I had fashioned a

Magus knew, and he thought often of the Diabolicon as he guided the Church of Satan.

THE TEMPLE OF SET

Whatever the circumstances, Michael Aquino left the Church of Satan on 10 June 1975 and formed the Temple of Set. He also had yet another document to justify his actions. He had become the Magus V degree that was formerly reserved for LaVey. He had become the rightful heir to the leadership of Satan/Set on earth. It was a power orchestrated in hell, the cosmos, or perhaps the creative genius of Michael Aquino.

Arguments concerning the schism within the Church of Satan are almost pointless. Some believe that LaVey lost his large following because he became too lax in the way in which he handled the membership and leadership. Others feel that Aquino was on a power trip and used his writings to find justification for his actions. A few point out that the Church of Satan was never very powerful, that LaVey was simply a great showman in his early days, something he has avoided of late in ceasing to give print interviews and make television and radio appearances.

Regardless of the reasons for the schism, Aquino's group is extremely small and less well known than his former mentor's church. This is justified by the idea that most humans are sheep, willing to subjugate their wills to God, so Aquino goes after only the gifted who are willing to free themselves from the constraints of the universe, claiming he does not want a large following. Yet just as he once would never have broken with LaVey, giving all honor and glory to the founder of the Church of Satan, it is hard to know what changes would be justified if large numbers of people showed a strong interest in the Temple of Set.

The members of the Temple of Set are probably a more intellectual group than adherents of the Church of Satan. The basic reading list of the Temple of Set is extremely broad, including both fiction and nonfiction with a healthy dose of reading on the Third Reich. These include such works as *The Occult and the Third Reich* by Jean-Michael Angebert; *Mein Kampf* by Adolf Hitler; *The War Path* and *Hitler's War*, both by David Irving; *Hitler's Table Talk 1941–1944* by H. R. Trevor-Roper; *Hitler's Secret Sciences* by Nigel Pennick; *Hitler: The Occult Messiah* by Gerald Suster; and numerous others.

The selected fiction is also interesting—such novels and short stories as those of Howard Phillips (H.P.) Lovecraft; *Rosemary's Baby* by Ira Levin; *The Omen* by David Seltzer; *Damien-Omen II* by Joseph Howard; *The Final Conflict* by Gordon McGill; *The Magus* by John Fowles; and numerous others. Some are movie novelizations.

In the case of *The Magus*, there are two different versions. The first is recommended, although Fowles has been quoted as saying that he wrote the second because almost no one, including himself, understood the first, which was poorly written.

The reading list for the members does provide a comprehensive study guide of books on everything from ancient Egyptian religion to modern satanic thought. Most of the books are annotated with comments about their quality and with reasons why they should be read. For example, Aquino justified the reading list by stating:

"An effective magician must be able to influence the fourth dimension as well as the first three. Such skill involves understanding and application of the principles which define and govern past periods of focus within the time-continuum, together with both passive analysis and active manipulation of the future."

In a letter to one of the authors, Aquino explained his belief in acquired knowledge as it related to the Temple of Set. He stated in part:

The configuration of a philosophy is not done overnight, and it is not done didactically. In my political theory courses I always stress the difference between "philosophy" and "ideology," recommending of course the former as a "disinterested search for truth" rather than the latter as a simplified sales pitch for a concept that may or may not be intrinsically sound. The Temple of Set is deliberately philosophical, hence we make every effort to avoid the pitfalls of ideology. Accordingly we can appear somewhat frustrating to people in a hurry, who want everything served to them in the kind of mental-fast-food format to which our rat-race yuppie culture has accustomed us. Aristotle spent 20 years as Plato's student before commencing to formulate his own philosophy.

Aquino has also discussed such concerns as the role of Christ and the idea of Greater Black Magic. When discussing Jesus, he has stated:

(1) Jesus maintained, per the Hebrew tradition, that humans are born into a state of 'original sin' from which they cannot escape save through him. Those who refused to accept him as savior would be damned to eternal punishment whether or not they were intentionally vicious persons. This doctrine resulted in (a) Christianity's being a religion backed ultimately by a threat and thus preying upon human fear, and (b) an excuse for human viciousness as long as it is done with religious sanction. Hence, the Crusades, Inquisitions, European religious wars, and maltreatment of non-Christians which have pervaded Christianity's history.

The statement has validity in a simplistic manner. Jesus stressed the necessity for finding his way in order to achieve eternal life. For example, in John 6:35–40, Jesus declared that he can satisfy the hunger of humanity as the bread of life or quench its thirst.

In Matthew 9:12–13, Jesus is quoted as saying, "It is not the healthy who need a doctor, but the sick. But go and learn what this means: 'I desire mercy, not sacrifice.' For I have not come to call the righteous, but sinners."

In the story of the adulterous woman, Jesus rebuked the judgmental in the crowd, "If any one of you is without sin, let him be the first to throw a stone at her" (John 8:7).

Those who reject the Lord may be denied access to God's kingdom, yet Jesus' message is one of the suffering servant bringing love, not vengeance. Those who have abused others in the name of Christ are not Christians; Jesus would never have tolerated such actions.

What Aquino ignores, in addition to the full teachings of Jesus, is the fact that many have suffered in the name of Satan. If Satan is not evil, as Aquino seems to feel, then what of the murders, the tortures, and the viciousness that have been committed in the name of Satan? Doesn't this make his beliefs ridiculous? Doesn't this reality simply show a rather one-sided and subjective view of Christianity? Despite Aquino's arguments, the teachings and life of Jesus may be opposite to the claims and lives of his followers.

Aquino continued:

> (2) Jesus insisted that other religions besides his not be tolerated. This evolved into an institutional policy of persecution of heretics and non-Christians, whether Jews, European pagans, native North/Central/South Americans, Islamics, agnostics, or atheists. Hence the torture and slaughter of accused 'witches' in medieval Europe, the slaughter & virtual extermination of entire races of people in the western hemisphere, and of course the waves of antisemitic pogroms culminating in the genocidal excesses of our own time.

Again, the assumption is that Christianity as taught by Jesus is responsible for the perversions of those who claim to be followers. Jesus is responsible for his teachings, not the corruption of his utterances. If Jayne Mansfield truly was murdered by people who felt the were carrying out the wishes of Anton LaVey, is LaVey guilty for their actions if he never knew they might take place? The excesses of people claiming to be Christians have nothing to do with the message of Christ. To class them together, then condemn the teacher, is a perversion of logical reasoning.

(3) Jesus held posthumous life to be superior to and more enduring than physical life. Christians are thus expected to qualify for the most comfortable afterlife by enduring various privations and abstinences in this life. Hence Christian humanity, to the extent it takes Christianity seriously and literally, enjoys natural life less than it might—for no better reason than superstition.

For these reasons I would say that Jesus, to the extent that he may have conceived these doctrines, has been the catalyst for an extraordinary amount of human suffering during the last 2,000 years. Has the non-Christian world fared much better? Probably not. But this in itself does not excuse Christianity's record.

Metaphysically I find no reason to think that Christianity is a true representation of the design or intelligence of the Universe. I have examined its "proofs" and found them illogical and/or insubstantial, and I have examined its "miracles" and found them mythical and meaningless. Hence I am no more concerned with Jesus as a "divine challenge" to the Temple of Set than I would be with the Easter Bunny or the Tooth Fairy.

This casual dismissal of Christianity from a man who holds himself to be a scholar and researcher is an interesting comment. In another letter 22 March 1985, Aquino admitted his ignorance in the area he has dismissed. He wrote:

I have not studied or evaluated Christianity as a biblical scholar, but rather as a social scientist. Hence I judge it by the effects I have observed it to have on human philosophy, politics, society, culture, and history. Since I do not think that Christianity's core cosmology is accurate, I have not spent much time delving through its internal writings—such as the Bible—any more than I have spent time studying Blavatsky's Secret Doctrine once I realized it to be a plagiarism of the Rig Veda. Sharpshooting the Bible in any number of ways has been the hobby of rationalists, atheists, etc. for some centuries now—and I have yet to see that it makes much difference. Those who believe in the book will continue to do so, and those who class it as just one more book of old legends and stories don't care about the technical flaws—any more than you or I worry about inconsistencies in the Tao Te Ching.

The area of Black Magic discussed by Aquino is probably one of the most important areas to understand. This is because it is the most feared by outsiders, Christians, and others. Some fear that a Satanist practicing lesser or greater Black Magic is capable of taking control of a person regardless of their attitude. A number of police officers, evidently fearful, have expressed reluctance to be involved with Satanist cases, yet these same officers claim to be Christians. Nothing in Christianity or the Bible indicates Satan can defeat God; nevertheless, the fear exists.

As Aquino stated in *The Crystal Tablet of Set:*

Lesser Black Magic is the influencing of beings, processes, or objects in the objective universe by the application of obscure physical or behavioral laws.
Lesser Black Magic is an impelling (encouraging, convincing, increasing of probability) measure, not a compelling (forcing, making inevitable) one. The object is to make something happen without expending the time and energy to make it happen through

direct cause and effect. In order to receive celebrity treatment in society, for example, one may work for many years to become a genuine celebrity. On the other hand, one may simply represent oneself outwardly as a celebrity, behave correspondingly, and receive much the same deference. One risks being exposed and embarrassed, but such risk is small if the magician is skillful in his assumed character.

All Lesser Black Magic is a variation on this basic theme. It involves everything from simple tricks of misdirection to extremely subtle and complex manipulation of psychological factors in the human personality. While it requires less time and effort in application than overt, direct methods, it is more intellectually demanding and requires extensive practice.

Later Aquino stated:

Greater Black Magic is the causing of change to occur in the subjective universe in accordance with the Will. The change in the subjective universe will cause a similar and proportionate change in the objective universe.

Examine this definition. A deliberate effort is made to alter one's subjective frame of reference, so that a thing that used to be conceptualized in one way is now conceptualized in another. A distasteful situation may be adjusted to produce a favorable outcome; a live enemy may be adjusted to be impaired or dead; a desire of any sort may be realized.

Manuals of magic from the medieval grimoires to the *Satanic Bible* have discussed the use of imagery as an aid to this conceptualization. Perhaps the most stereotypical example of this is the sticking of pins into a wax effigy to cause harm. In Walt Disney's *Dumbo* the little elephant was given a feather to hold with his trunk; he was told that it was a magic feather which would enable him to fly—and he did so by flapping his ears. When he eventually lost the feather, he started to fall, until he was told that the feather was nothing more than an ordinary feather. As soon as he realized this, he flapped his ears again and regained altitude.

> Photographs, wax images, talismans, music, fires, swords, statues, and indeed entire ritual chambers have no more intrinsic magic in them than Dumbo's feather. Their effectiveness in magic, again like Dumbo's feather, comes from their significance to the magician. If he grants them certain powers in his subjective universe—if he credits them with atmospheres, auras, curses, or blessings—they will assuredly have them. They will possess these qualities absolutely in the subjective universe. Once this occurs, the phenomenon of the Magical Link between the subjective and objective universes will transfer a portion of the quality to the items' objective mass. The potency and endurance of the transfer depends upon the skill and Will power of the magician, the scope of the Working, the amount of distortion in the objective universe attempted, and a wide variety of physical and environmental factors which may range from a sore toe which intrudes upon the magician's concentration to sunspot activity.

There is obviously more to Black Magic as defined by Aquino, though the quotes provide the general information. It is also not something sanctioned with innocents around. In the section related to preparing the chamber for working, he stated:

> Children should not be allowed to attend any Working of Greater Black Magic. They will not understand it, may be frightened by it, and may wrongly represent it to others. Pets may be present only if they can be depended upon to enhance, not disrupt the atmosphere. Under no conditions is any life-form ever sacrificed or injured in a Black Magic Working of the Temple of Set. Violation of this rule

111

will result in the offender's immediate expulsion and referral to law enforcement or animal protection authorities.

SET FOLLOWERS

What does all this mean? Essentially, the follower of the Temple of Set might be described as an intellectual hedonist. No matter what Aquino may claim or actually follow when screening his members, the appeal, with both the Temple of Set and the Church of Satan, lies in the justification of personal goals over community values.

Essentially the main difference between Christianity and such groups as the Temple of Set and the Church of Satan is that Christ was the suffering servant. He stressed working for the good of others rather than for the pleasure of one's self. He also taught certain restrictions on individual action for a greater good.

For example, monogamy is not a trait that is of particular importance among Satanism or the Temple of Set. It is a value that may be right for one person, wrong for another, and both situations are okay so long as the individual involved is happy. Christianity stresses the strength of the relationship between two people. It is a religion of commitment, not self-pleasure. Sometimes sacrifice must be made for the greater good, though that doesn't mean Christianity is a religion without pleasure.

For example, neither Christ's teachings nor Paul's letters indicates that being rich is sinful or will keep someone from heaven. The teachings do not support the idea, professed by some Christians, that only poverty buys your way into heaven. They also do not support the idea that God wants us all to prosper and have wealth. Instead, they condemn only the pursuit of wealth as a goal unto itself. When wealth becomes the ultimate achievement, valued to such a degree that no goal is as important as maintaining that wealth, then it is wrong. The key is the rich person's attitude about wealth.

With the Satan/Set teachings, any goal that is personally desirable is generally justifiable. It is a self-centered, fairly elitist attitude that holds "good works" in disdain unless such works are the personal choice of the individual. The idea of sharing with the less fortunate because it is right or because that is how you would wish to be treated if the situation was reversed is not considered. And in the extreme, it gives justification for the acts of the deranged, just as some men and women take pride in "killing for Christ."

Michael Aquino's military connection is obviously of concern. Prior to making lieutenant colonel, he wrote to one of the authors, explaining:

> My first exposure to the Army was via high school ROTC, wherein I rose to the top rank of Cadet Colonel. I went on to college ROTC at the University of California, received an ROTC scholarship from the Department of the Army, and was commissioned as a Distinguished Graduate in the Regular Army in 1968. I have since become qualified in Airborne, Special Forces (the "Green Berets"), Psychological Operations, Strategic Intelligence, and Defense Attache fields. My primary specialty is "Politico-Military Affairs Officers," and I am a member of the Foreign Area Officer career program. I served a tour in Vietnam in 1969–70, receiving the Bronze Star, Air Medal, and Army Commendation Medal for my work there. I am a graduate of several courses at the JFK Special Warfare Center, the Command & General Staff College, the Defense Intelligence College, the Armor School, the Intelligence School, and the State Department's Foreign Service Institute.

Psychological operations have been a favorite of Aquino. This interest, a logical extension of his Black Magic studies, raises the question of how far he might go to influence civilians either in time of war or peace. Although one might expect the military to inquire about his relations with the

Temple of Set, Aquino has been relatively left alone. Other officers have had problems.

For example, in 1971, one officer wrote to Aquino with a problem he was having with the military. This man, then a warlock in the Church of Satan and later an active member of the Temple of Set before becoming disenchanted and leaving, wrote:

> I have just discovered that the introduction of institutional Satanism to the military establishment does indeed open some Pandora's boxes, as you put it in your letter of August 23rd.
>
> Things have gone well here lately, and I have interested several people in the Church. It was my intention to place an article in the base newspaper this week, but that has occurred which is forcing a drastic revision of my promotional plans.
>
> Yesterday I went before a promotion board, having served time in grade to be eligible for promotion to corporal. With the promotion I would find the door open to a new social stratum, a privately-owned vehicle, a little more money ... but I have been forced to "fall back and regroup."
>
> The board refused to recommend me for promotion. One reason given was that I was still not displaying enough initiative and aggressiveness until a couple of months ago, though they admitted I have improved greatly in that respect since then. True enough: I have found it difficult until recently to motivate myself to a high standard of performance within a system I find so repressive and restricting. Realizing, however, that an adept Satanist is versatile enough to succeed in whatever circumstances he finds himself, I have taken corrective action—though a little late.
>
> The core of the matter, however, was the fact that I am a Satanist. The board openly admitted that it was

the main reason I was not being promoted. Their reasoning was as follows:

I work as a security guard in a confinement facility. Through leaks from other duty personnel the confinees long ago became aware of my religious affiliation, and are constantly asking about it. I try to discourage this by simply refusing to discuss the matter, but as the old confinees tell the new ones about me the cycle continues. Thus, they concluded that my being a Satanist is detrimental to my effectiveness in a rehabilitation program. I was told I could not expect to be promoted until Satanism was proven to be no longer an obstacle to the effective performance of my duty: i.e., "recant or you'll never advance."

They were also disturbed that I had been talking about Satanism to other Marines, though I made it perfectly clear that I have never discussed it with anyone who did not first ask me for information about it. I was cautioned against proselytizing and was told, "The Marine Corps is not a recruiting ground for Satanism. Take it underground." When they asked how many Marines had ever witnessed the Satanic rites they had heard about from everyone (except myself) and I truthfully replied, "none," they said, "Keep it that way."

I was also told that Satanism, differing as it does from other religions, is "eccentric," and eccentricity is an undesirable quality in a Marine non-commissioned officer. Again they said, in effect, that as long as I am a Satanist I cannot expect to be promoted.

I am not at all certain that all this is legal. What they said is true enough for the most part, but I do not feel that it is right for them to hold me back because of my religion.

I feel certain that if I were to write my Congressman some action would be taken, but I fear that such a course of action would in the long run cause more harm than good, both to me and to the Church: we need publicity, but *not* notoriety.

I appear to have two choices at this point: I can "go underground," which would make the establishment of a grotto here a long and tedious process indeed; or, I can attempt to maneuver myself into a situation in which I will have a little more freedom of action. I intend to try the latter first by arranging through proper channels to see my executive officer, explain the situation, and request that I be transferred to another unit on base. This would ordinarily be difficult, as corrections is my M.O.S., but I think I can do it, considering the circumstances. Besides, I am qualified in other areas. I could go into Special Services as a karate instructor (I am a former civilian instructor and black belt holder) or, preferably, I could work in disbursing, as I was in banking before I joined the corps.

The letter ended by explaining that the situation might resolve itself. However, if it did not, he wanted to alert Michael Aquino because he might need assistance or advice.

The end result was that the soldier eventually went on to rise in the military. The Church of Satan is a legally recognized entity in the United States; to violate the rights of a member, regardless of someone else's beliefs, would be in conflict with the First Amendment guarantee that Congress will make no law affecting the freedom of religion.

It is interesting to note that when the soldier eventually left the Temple of Set years later, he reflected upon his past in a series of exclusive interviews. By then he was hostile to Aquino, and his words have to be taken in that light. He spoke of what he felt was a pro-Nazi bias on the part of Aquino and some of his followers. He felt that many of the teachings were without validity. And he also felt that most of what he blamed on Black Magic might have been from other things.

For example, he told of how he was almost fired from a bank

because one official did not personally like his religious beliefs. He claimed that his work record did not warrant it, but he had no recourse because of his low position.

The night before the man was to discuss the planned dismissal with his supervisor, he performed a destruction ritual. The ritual was designed to take the life of the bank official, though he revealed his actions to no one. Then, the next day, the official dropped dead from a massive heart attack as he was hurrying to work. The man was able to retain his job until he voluntarily left banking to join the Marines.

The man was thrilled when he heard the news, paying homage to Satan the way a Christian or Jew would thank God for blessings received. However, after he left the group he began reflecting on the experience. He realized that the official was in his fifties, grossly overweight, had a terrible diet, smoked constantly, and was under intense stress for the previous several weeks. Just the stress related to the firing might have caused the heart attack. After leaving Satanism, he realized that he had not really seen its dark side. In large measure, he had been a part of what might be considered black theater.

TWO WENT TO PREY

So what does it all mean? What influence have Michael Aquino and Anton LaVey had on Satanism in the United States? For that matter, are they Satan/Set anointed, with special powers and abilities far beyond those of mortal men (said with apologies to Superman)?

The answer is that both men have less influence than perhaps they themselves would like to believe. Of the two, Anton LaVey is the more important on a national scale. His *Satanic Bible* and the showmanship that has made him famous have encouraged many people, some of whom are deranged, to begin acting in the name of Satan. He has made the socially unacceptable more acceptable. He has helped make Satanism and Devil worship a topic for home conversa-

117

tion. No matter how serious he may be, no matter what powers he may have developed, it is the image even more than the substance that has had such a strong influence on individuals throughout the nation.

Michael Aquino's role is less obvious. From his writings, he must be considered the most important representative of Satan/Set on earth. Yet his followers are few, his name not widely known, and the way the major writings that flow from his hand seem to interpret life and religion in his image, not necessarily reality, makes him a figure of curiosity.

What matters is that Aquino's being in an ever higher military capacity is a worrisome specter. Just as extremists of any sort are to be feared in positions of power and influence, so is the issue of Michael Aquino in the military a concern. By constitutional declaration, his beliefs are sacred and his life may not be violated because of them. This reality should not be changed because he would have an equal case for banning Christianity from the military. Yet he is a concern for which there is no answer.

As a civilian, it might be easy to find Michael Aquino's arrogance and practices almost amusing. Likewise, if Anton LaVey had never written *The Satanic Bible,* he could be considered an eccentric showman. But Aquino is in the military and LaVey did write his book. As a result, their influence, in one form or another, greatly exceeds the relative handful of people who actively hold membership in either group.

DEVILRY

DEVIL-GAMES: DUNGEONS & DRAGONS?

His name is not important. He might have been anyone's brother, anyone's son. He lived in the Denver, Colorado area, a place where more than twenty similar stories would be told in the two years following his death. And similar stories have been heard in Ohio, Arizona, Florida, California, Washington State, and elsewhere. Some say they are not connected. Others say they are the results of an insidious plot by a game designer seeking to fulfill a pact with Satan. But what is known is a story of a young mind beginning a journey through a maze of fantasy, isolation, and ultimate madness.

THE ESSENCE OF TRAGEDY

He was fourteen when it started, a boy of brilliance, a faithful churchgoer, an honor student, a youth who was the type parents delighted in seeing come to their house because he was such a good influence on others. Everyone knew he would attend college, marry, raise a family, and be an asset to the community.

When I was young good and evil was put to me with fire and brimstone. The thought of evil sent shivers up my spine. No matter how bad I talked or how bad I acted, there was no question that evil was wrong.

The vehicle for his decline seemed innocent enough— Dungeons & Dragons, a fantasy game in which the players created powers and strategies to help them win. It was more popular than many other fantasy games at the time and slightly different only in that the bad guy had a better chance of winning. Characters with evil, violent powers generally had more points and were able to stay alive longer. Thus most beginning players chose to claim for themselves the powers of the damned. It was a little like watching the old west gun fight at high noon, hoping that the man in the black hat will not only shoot the man in the white hat, but he will kidnap his victim's wife, rape her, then steal what had been their home.

Note on the creation of the character who would represent him in the game of Dungeons & Dragons: *After serious contemplation I have finally entitled myself as Maskim Xul. There is no joyfilled laughter in mine ear. No love in mine heart. Just hatred burning hot in my veins. Day after day I pray for the damnation of mankind. And with the coming of night I rejoice in the horrified screams of people as I thrust my hideous weapon into their bodies. Tearing them open untill they are nothing but a pile of lifeless and bleeding flesh. My mercies are none. For I am he who dwells in gloom. Finding sanctuary in the dark bowls of the earth, I am the beast that growls in pain. And I will avenge myself untill my thurst for blood has been apeased! So heed to my words, all who may listen. I walk a path that only Metaxul has dared venture. And unless you are he, from this moment on live your life in terror.*

The odd twist in the game, the need for a player to be evil in order to have the best chance of winning, was contrary to every other popular game in the previous century; yet that did not make it satanic. Dungeons & Dragons, like all the other fantasy games, is an amusement, a diversion, a way to expand the mind. Tragically, for some children it is also an obsession, a way of life in which fantasy and reality blend to the point where it is difficult to discern which is which. When that occurs, they begin to wonder if the powers they discuss have a basis in reality. And if they do, can we mortals take control of them and use them for our personal ends?

But as I grew, evil became more and more a part of my life. I found that I had a definite evil about me. But it went to extremes. For the most part I was extremely good and truthful. I had a good knowledge about life and human nature. At times, though, the evil came out in full force. And when it did it was almost caotic.

This evil only came about in times of anger or when I was scared. But it grew, and soon it came out at any time.

There was still an imbalance. Good still outnumbered the evil. And I hadn't become aware of it yet. Ignorance made my body a perfect ally for it.

I Maskim Xul was born in the 6th month on the 6th day in the year 66. I bear the number of the beast! From the beginning of my existence I lied and stole for my enjoyment. At an early age I planned rape and murder. My mind has always been cluttered with "evil" thoughts. And who is my lofty maker? No one I say! It is I who hath made me what I am today! And it is I who will decide my fate! So it is this that I profess, tomorrow I will be eviler than I was today! And with the coming of each night, my mind will be writtled with caotic disorder.

The changes in him were slow in coming, little different from those experienced by most adolescents, at least on the surface. His room had been covered with posters, primarily with images of models in bathing suits. Puberty had struck and, with it, the normal obsessions of youth.

Yet gradually his life became different enough to be a curiosity to his parents. Taken down were the posters of the attractive young women that once decorated his walls. In their place were posters and drawings of monsters and mythological creatures. Although friends still came to play, the ones whose interests were greater than just playing endless rounds of fantasy games began visiting less and less. It was as though he was withdrawing into a world where fantasy was more important than the reality he was experiencing.

In retrospect, his parents realized that they probably should have gotten more involved with their son, but they knew from their friends that all teenagers have a tendency to withdraw from their parents. And on the surface, he still seemed to enjoy family activities, camping, church. What they could not see was the hurt taking place inside, a hurt he never expressed, even to his closest friends. The only indication of his internal struggle came from his diary.

I feel so alone in this bustling world. Such as a deaf child in the city. I am within reach of reality, but it happens without pity. Here and there comeing in contact but always falling behind. A prisoner trapped within the depths of a torn and forgotten mind. Escapes are few just to be thrown back to my lonely place. And just when I think I am shareing with others, I am scourged to this isolated place. Crazy am I not. The world happens as through a door ajar and my sences sharpen, and it is all understood. Though answers are far.

It is hard to say what was happening inside his mind. He began reading books about fantasy, mythology, and the occult. He discovered that there were book stores devoted to mysticism, witchcraft, Satanism, and similar practices. He began browsing in them when his parents would be unaware of his

124

activities. And sometime during this period, his mind began to change, his feelings intensified, his anger grew. . . .

As time passed I became quite aware of the beast within me. But I regarded it with indifference. I still was more good than evil.

People started to push me. More and more, they tormented me and several times in fits of anger I looked to evil for help.

Now the balance was equal! It expanded without mercy. I had a choice and began to look to "evil" more than good.

Lonely, despite loving parents who would have reached out to him if he had expressed what was in his heart, he began looking for ways to change. During one of the games, a friend called upon Satan as a way of winning. He asked for satanic powers, and he won the game.

His winning was a curiosity. Satan couldn't be real, he thought. Satan had no interest in becoming involved with a game of fantasy.

Or was he real? What would happen if someone truly embraced the dark side of life? Would the powers of the game become powers for the experiences of daily life?

He had to know. If Satan was not a reality, then selling your soul would be but a game. If Satan was a reality, then perhaps the powers of darkness could change his life and bring him happiness. Quietly, in his bedroom, he took a piece of paper and he wrote:

I give to the Lord Lucifer, my soul, and twenty others within 30 years, for the listed powers:

1. The power of invisability.

2. The power of polymorf (shape change).

3. Time stop.

4. The power to fly.

5. The power to levitate.

6. The power to cast Hell fire and beams of energy forth from my hand at any instance.

And then he signed his name, an action as solemn and serious as if he had shared blood with the Devil himself.

The games changed, at least so far as his notebooks were concerned. Class notes were mingled with papers that held drawings of daggers, blood, and mythological beasts. He put together a shopping list for a ritual, a list that included:

Altar
6 black candles
acursed chalis
black robe
bell
symbols (2 major, others trivial)
1 cup of blood (if required)
podeum
insence burner
powder of life
staff.

His actions with the games also took on a more bizarre twist. For example, one of his notes read:

I call to thee, oh acursed one. Awaken from your eternal slumber. Rise from the firey pit of Hell. For you are the "evil" one, the lost child, the one who's wrampant rath once spread terror among your kind. By my words rise and live again. My voice is wraped in rolling thunder so that you may hear these words.

And always his diary chronicled his change.

Occasionally the "evil" would retreat deep within the confines of my body. Turning me into a benign lover of life, but not for long, that unspeakable horror was soon to rise. And it did.

Growing strong the horned beast was taking me over. Then I realized this beast was me! I was the "evil", I was growing, spreading, multiplying. I am this foul aparation scourge to a human body.

He was declining, his mind sinking slowly into madness. He had become unable to tell the difference between fantasy and reality. To some, he might seem to have been possessed, at least in retrospect. To others he was a severely disturbed youth. But at the time, a friend described him best, saying: "He was always smiling and laughing and seemingly happy. In all the time I knew him, I was never able to get in touch with his real feelings deep inside, and I feel badly now that I didn't try harder."

He also wrote of his troubles and his growing obsession, not just with evil but with fantasy as a substitute for reality. He said: "The only escape is to retreat from the physical world into the visionary depths of the mind and enjoy visions of inner reality."

And somewhere in the midst of the games, his school, his friends, his growing isolation from his family, somewhere in the slow decline of a brilliant mind, he slipped over into what he perceived to be insanity.

Madman! Ah, yes, this is the name I have entitled upon myself. Such a loathsome name, such a horrid thing to be envisioned as, but such is the reality that has overpowered me. How I would of trembled, with fear running cold through my veins. How my blood would have thickened and my skin crawled, with beads of sweat pouring forth from my body, if I had only known the terrible fate that was planned for me.

This is gone now. I used to fear the thought of total insanity, but now it is welcome, almost cherished. How I used to sit up at night and plan my terrible deeds, laughing insanely until the dark hours of the night. Creeping through the darkness was my thing. I used to lurk in the still night. Crawling upon a neighbors doorstep, watching and waiting. Oh they were happy times.

As madness began to overtake me, I had a certain uneasiness. Caught between fantasy and reality, I dreaded the outcome. How would people look upon a creature of insanity? Pointing and leering, they would scourge me to a place of seclusion. But . . . , who was to know! The more I lost touch with reality, the more cunning I became. This was the answer. My secret would be known only to myself.

The idea of Satanism soon became an obsession. Under the guise of going to a movie, he and another would visit an occult bookstore near the theater and browse until just before their parents came to pick them up. Their deception was never discovered.

He would write:

Mingling in the cosmos had always been my thing, and I had soon become satanically involved. This excited me, I had found great success in evil and good turned out to be nothing more than a sham.

Soon I rejected the traditional Catholic goal of God and Jesus Christ. I deny all their prayers [next two words unclear] and rites. I pledge my allegiance to the Lord Satan, and follow along the left hand path. My morals are gone, I have no feeling for humanity. Each day I pray for the damnation of mankind. My mind and its monstrous thoughts have become inhuman. Sanity is not the question. I'm as sane as the next though my views reap great harm in the minds of others my cause is known. I do not claim to be as the next for I am one of a kind. My decayed mind will forever be wridled with "evil." But I am reality.

The crossover between game and life was complete with game words and life thoughts mingling together. He felt pressured to take the blood that his character feasted upon. His words became more horrible, fantasy and reality blending into a nightmare existence locked within his mind.

People; I hate people. I loath people. I can barely withstand their very existence. They are insecure and feeble minded. All they do is get in the way. I laugh with ecstasy at the thought of making one bleed. People are inferior to me, for I have become almost inhuman. As I sit, I pray for their downfall and destruction. Some day I will be rid of them all!

Until then, to kill and destroy is my only thought.

I give to thee, your life to keep; If you pass and let me sleep; But if thou dare go below the stones; Death to he who moves my bones.

By day I am forced to walk with the living. By night I am he who communes with the dead.

Tragically, this is not the story of a monster but of a good boy, one of hundreds around the country who have become disturbed through their obsession with fantasy, using games as a way to venture into a world more horrible than they could originally imagine.

He could not hurt, yet he was driven to violence. His actions belied his words; his rage, his pain, his inner drive for blood were all countered by his inability to act upon his feelings. His troubled mind told him to commit murder; his heart told him he could not. He found that writing poetry staved off his blood lust, yet he realized that suicide might be the only way to keep from hurting family, friends, or strangers.

They say there is a separate peace,
Now I have found my own;
for when the time of passing is near,
It is better left unknown,
Unto the depths of Hell I'm cast,
Never to see the future, and all because of the Past;
It is not death that makes me weep,
But the life that was [word unclear] for me,
It was one that I could keep.

Life is like a big glass ball
With future in its [word unclear]
People playing catch with it, trying to break this precious
mold
One slip here One slip there
This mold will break in two
And so ends the future of the one and only you.

It was two years from his first involvement before he felt his own death was inevitable. He gave no warning signs to his family, his friends, or his teachers other than his declining grades, yet even this situation was not all that unusual. Adolescence is a troubled time at best. Puberty, changing interests and body chemistry, and other factors often result in moody, daydreaming students.

What was important, the diary, his drawings, even ritual objects such as daggers he had purchased were all so carefully hidden that even a prying mother would probably not have found them. He used hollowed out books for many of his treasures, his actions were furtive, his pact with Satan too personal for him to want anyone to discover the truth.

And finally there came the day when he sat down to write for the last time—a tragic farewell that could only have been stopped had he chosen to reach out to someone else.

Upon reading these words you will know that I am dead. I have now started the lonesome journey to the bowels of the earth. I travel that twisted road that winds its way down to the forsaken pit. It is time to meet my lofty maker! My destination will be the foot of the throne, where I will kneel and greet my father. Thus, ending my travel. Wearily I will scale the great monument, and seat myself by the side of my lord. Bowing my head in shame for I had not the strength nor the courage to continue my earthly existence. Though I am a shamefull sight, my father will spread his wings and welcome me to his, and my real home.

Though I am dead, I am kept alive by the reading of these words. But upon reading the last, I will just be a memory. So let these last moments be true and sincere.

My death is one that could of been avoided. I could have lived for a long time here with you. Building the foundation for my future existence. But something went wrong. My sences began to sharpen rapidly and to live became a discomfort. I was caught between the hatred for this world and the thirst for blood. My plite for "evil" became stagnant. The only instinct was to act, and act fast. So, ending my life.

He finished the note, went to the garage, closed the door, and started the engine of the car. His mother was grocery shopping and would not return for at least an hour. His father was at work. By the time the youth was discovered, the accumulation of carbon monoxide gas within the garage had taken its toll. The boy was dead.

There are more questions than answers about not only his death but also the deaths of others. In the Denver area alone, more than twenty deaths were linked to similar circumstances. Although it is unusual for someone to leave such a dramatic record of his or her experience, the experience itself is frighteningly common.

Some critics blame fantasy games and, more specifically, Dungeons & Dragons. They say it is satanic, that the creator sold his soul to Satan and is using the game to corrupt the youth of the nation. Defenders say that it is just a game, no different from any other except for the fact that evil frequently triumphs over good.

Whatever the truth, the one unavoidable reality is that a number of impressionable, often highly intelligent young minds are becoming obsessed with fantasy games to a degree that can be detrimental to their emotional health. Any form of obsession is dangerous, including when someone is so obsessed with the Bible that they commit acts of violence in the name of God.

The desire for power, for control, for the ability to achieve what no mortal has accomplished is a major reason why many people enter Satanism. As you have seen and will see in the rest of this book, the desire for fame, money, adoration from the opposite sex, or the avoidance of the unpleasant aspects of life are all reasons for Satan worship by adults. It is thus understandable how an impressionable teenager, playing a fantasy game, might decide that magical powers are real.

The tragedy of the contemporary fantasy games has been some players' violent deaths. The Ouija Board, a game designed to place the players in touch with the spirit world, also has been used by many converts to Satanism. The difference has been the intent. With a Ouija Board, the individuals who wanted to explore metaphysics, Satanism, and similar pursuits did so consciously. Often they saw the board as a vehicle towards achieving this end.

The appeal of the fantasy games is more seductive. Often the intention for playing was no more than spending a pleasant afternoon in creative play. In fact, a number of schools around the country are using games such as Dungeons & Dragons to stimulate creative thinking. Should a child become obsessed, should the child begin to see the game as a vehicle for achieving power through Satan worship, the clues may come too late for parents and friends to alter the course of a potential tragedy.

A TIME TO KILL

In contrast to the cases of obsession with Dungeons & Dragons is the story of Sean Sellers, a teenager who, at this writing, lives on death row in the Oklahoma State Penitentiary. Sellers murdered his mother and his father, and a convenience store clerk. He was also an avid fan of Dungeons & Dragons, but other factors in his childhood may have been much more important in his choosing the path of Satanism.

Psychologists and psychiatrists generally agree that the stresses of early childhood can become the explosive violence of adolescence. A child who is emotionally and physically battered may be withdrawn but may seem "perfect," polite, helpful, doing whatever is asked. Yet body chemistry changes affect emotions. In the extreme, a teenager can vent his or her rage in an orgy of death.

This may have been the case with Sean Sellers. His parents were divorced when he was a year-and-a-half-old. His mother, Vonda, had difficulty finding work during the next eighteen months, so she decided to leave Sean and seek employment in another city.

Sean was cared for by a succession of relatives, apparently never getting close to any of them no matter how hard he tried. He apparently felt abandoned, a feeling that was made worse when his mother remarried.

Vonda married Paul Bellofatto, a mechanic who decided to switch professions and become a truck driver. Vonda agreed to accompany him on his cross-country hauls, again leaving Sean with family members.

Besides the problem of abandonment, Sean couldn't gain his parents' approval according to those who knew the family. No matter what he did, he could not meet their standards. Prior to adolescence he seemed withdrawn though well mannered. He was timid yet desired acceptance.

When Sean was in the seventh grade and his family had settled in an Oklahoma City suburb, he probably made his first friend—Jim Lofting, a boy who was raised by his grandparents. The two youths shared a fondness for sports, especially track, football, and weight lifting, as well as the game of Dungeons & Dragons.

In 1983, everything seemed to fall apart for Sean. His stepfather found a job in Greeley, Colorado, creating yet another move. A summer romance with a girl he met in a church camp did not last into the winter. Sean, depressed by the loss of his friends, the renewed upheaval, and the other pressures he was experiencing, considered suicide, then turned to Satanism. He later wrote in a journal he maintained: "Deep down I want power . . . the unruling power of the supernatural."

It was in 1984 that Sean became totally immersed in Satanism. His mother and stepfather returned to cross-country driving, and Sean was placed with Vonda's sister in Okulgee, Oklahoma. Instead of trying to fit in with yet more strangers in school, he turned to drinking and studying Satanism.

He and a friend went so far as to conduct a Satanic baptism with another boy during a visit to Colorado.

The one, naked except for a white sheet, was cut enough so Sean and his friend could have blood to drink. The boys performing the ceremony dressed in black, lit candles, and had both a silver chalice and a ritual sword. It was the foray of a troubled youth into a world that would grow increasingly violent for him.

It was February of 1985 when Sean took a blood oath to Satan. Alone in his bedroom with candles for light and incense for atmosphere, he cut himself, then used the blood to write "I renounce God, I renounce Christ, I will serve only Satan . . . Hail Satan."

Sean's personality had now changed entirely. Once he had been an honor-roll student, clean-cut, and as outgoing as a semi-loner can be when constantly changing schools. Now he stopped participating in sports, slacked off on his studies, and stopped taking an interest in his appearance. Frequently his dress was similar to those of the ninjutsu, the Japanese assassins. He also had *The Satanic Bible* at school and an altar for the black arts at home in his bedroom. Nothing was the same, yet no one knew quite how to help him.

Sean's stepfather was frustrated and irate. He denounced his son, allegedly telling him, "You do not exist." It was so troubling a statement that Sean withdrew to his books on Satanism.

The involvement with Satanism was so intense that Sean's

mother felt she was in a struggle for her son. His hostility towards his parents was intense, and his mother felt that he was determined to kill or destroy her in some way. Whether she sensed the murder to come or just was frightened by the boy's hostility is unknown. Vonda wrote to a cousin, saying, "Why my complete destruction is so important I don't know, unless it's because Satan knows I don't intend to give him up without a fight. To be honest I'm scared, but I'm reading the Bible and praying for help. . . ."

For Sean, Satanism seemed to become a way of life because it brought him attention and countered the values of his parents, who he felt had rejected him. His anger over his stepfather's denunciation was overwhelming. His mother's love was not enough, especially with his feelings of abandonment. His actions seemed a cry for attention.

Schoolwork changed radically. Sean made a show of going to visit with a Catholic priest and even attended a Bible study class at the request of his mother. But most of his actions were designed to shock, including biting off the leg of a live frog in biology class and carrying a vial of blood to drink in the cafeteria. Friends were almost nonexistent, but the other students were keenly aware of this troubled youth.

Sean's outrageous actions began attracting others. He regularly attended the cult movie *The Rocky Horror Picture Show* and spent much of his time in occult bookstores. He added to his different appearance by always wearing his left shirtsleeve rolled up and keeping the nail of the little finger of his left hand painted black.

The result was that Sean was seen as either a repulsive figure, a joke, or a serious leader, depending upon how impressionable fellow students happened to be. Gradually he gained several followers who formed their own version of a coven. They used an abandoned farmhouse for rituals and frequently drank blood. He also kept several refrigerated vials at home.

The more Sean's parents were horrified by his actions, the

more intense they became. He began writing a book filled with rituals for invoking spirits and demons. He began using stimulants to stay up all night so that he could study rituals; then he relied upon marijuana and alcohol to calm his body enough to rest.

He slept less and less, his mind focusing only on the satanic. Experts in psychosis feel that the sleep deprivation and constant thoughts on the satanic radically altered his personality. He reported periods of blackouts and an alter ego named Ezurate, a demon who would use Sean's body for evil.

In order to better prepare himself for Satan, Sean decided to break each of the Ten Commandments. When he got to "You shall not murder" is unknown. What is certain is that his first murder took place on September 8, 1985. At that time he and a friend went to a convenience store, determined to gain revenge against Robert Bower, a clerk who had refused to sell them beer. They were underage, but that did not matter to Sean. He had been humiliated and defied. Bower must die.

The death apparently was quick. Sean stole a .357 Magnum revolver from his grandfather, went to the store, aimed the gun, fired, and missed. The second shot caught Bower just as the clerk turned to flee the store. The wound did not slow him, but a third shot rang out before he could get more than a few yards. He fell dead.

Sean was not a suspect in Bower's death, a fact that may have reinforced his plunging himself even more deeply into Satanism. If a crime is committed and the person is not caught, the person may presume that he or she has special satanic protection. In reality, without a known motive for Bower's death, law enforcement officers had no reason to look for Sean or even know about his existence. Yet how Sean perceived his escape from the law is uncertain. What is known is that he plunged himself even deeper into his studies.

Sean obtained a job as a bouncer for a teenage nightclub, one of whose patrons was a fifteen-year-old girl named Angel. He claims that it was Ezurate who was drawn to the young woman's sexuality. Yet eventually Sean found himself thinking of nothing but Satanism or Angel, a girl of whom his parents disapproved.

Eventually Sean began to run away. He was miserable with his parents, his school, even the few followers of his "coven." One option was for him to go and live with his real father and the woman his father had recently married. But Paul and Vonda had custody, and they were against such a move. Once again they felt that strict behavior controls were what was needed, an attitude that increased the hostility already existing among them.

Yet always Sean was crying out for help, giving clues to his feelings and beliefs. A high school English teacher notified his parents of a composition that said, in part, "Satanism made me a better person. I am free. I can kill without remorse. . . ." They were frightened, concerned, yet all his mother could do was write him a note expressing her love. It was a note he would not see before they died.

What happened next is unclear. Sean was aware of some actions, but claims he blacked out during others. All that is certain is that he came home from a pizza parlor where he worked part-time, put on black underwear and a black-hooded cape. Then he made a makeshift altar with candles, incense, and a chalice of blood. He also obtained a .44 caliber revolver from his stepfather, though how he obtained it was not something he remembered. He may have sneaked it that night, or he may have taken it several days earlier, hiding it in his room until it was time for the murders.

Finally Sean entered his parents' bedroom, moving silently until he pointed the gun at his stepfather's head and pulled the trigger. He swung the gun to his mother's head and fired again. Unlike with the store clerk, he didn't miss this time.

With the blood, gore, hair, and bits of skull from his parents' murders splattered against the wall, Sean left the house. He went to spend the night with the friend with whom he had gone to the convenience store, and apparently slept well. The next day he returned home, "discovered" the corpses, and ran hysterically to a neighbor's home to call for the ambulance.

No immediate evidence implicated Sean, but both friends and family were certain of Sean's guilt. Vonda's father requested that Sean be a major suspect, so certain was he of the troubled youth's ability to kill.

Sean at first proclaimed his innocence and a lack of memory of the murder. Later, after being given the death sentence, he came to see himself as having a dual personality—Ezurate and Sean. Finally he turned to Christianity, studying the Bible, and talking with others about the Lord.

Yet the future for Sean is uncertain. He is on death row. He recognizes the reasons the government has given him the death penalty, and he accepts the full responsibility for having committed the murders. Although there are appeals at this writing, the future for him is unknown.

MAGNIFICENT OBSESSION

Two boys took lives, one only his own and the other a number of lives, but both were obsessed with a fantasy game. What does this say about Dungeons & Dragons and the related fantasy games that are such a concern today? No one knows. Many parents feel uncomfortable with any game requiring a player to be evil to win. Others see the obsession with the game as being the evil and not the game itself.

Some critics say that the two boys are the tips of icebergs and that many other children are being corrupted by fantasy games. Yet this is no different than saying that the violence of Saturday morning cartoons has created a nation of tiny monsters, waiting anxiously to be armed so they can do harm to one another.

For some children, a fantasy game becomes a real pursuit of power and its rewards. But could these children become equally obsessed with the Bible if brought to it in the same manner? Are the children who kill for Satan in his clutches from the games? Or are these not much different from the ones who kill in the name of Jesus, religious fanatics who tolerate no deviation from their disturbed mindset?

The answers, though generally unknown, do lead to at least one conclusion. Obsessive behavior in any manner can be destructive for both the young and the rest of us. It is this obsessive behavior that must be curbed by parents. Children may be misusing Dungeons & Dragons as well as similar fantasy games. But likewise, parents often encourage such play, just as they sometimes use the television set as an electronic baby-sitter. The games themselves do not seem to be a pathway to Satan. Rather, it is the abdication of parental involvement, the acceptance of what may be a warning sign of trouble, and similar factors that are the realities of these serious problems.

DEVIL-SONGS: ROCK & ROLL?

It began in the 1960s, a time of turmoil and contradictions. Some were trying to make the world a better place in which to live by marching in the streets, protesting injustice against blacks, working for social reforms, and standing against or for the Vietnam War. They felt that one person could change nothing, but people together could make a better world. They were for love in the truest sense, willing to give up their careers, their educations, even their lives for their fellow humans.

Other activists in the 1960s were the self-centered individuals, the ones seeking pleasure over any other experience. They filled the coffee shops, smoking marijuana, sipping wine, listening to folk music, jazz, or something more esoteric. They belonged to the "if it feels good, do it" school of life. Some were using sex, drugs, and their dropout mentality to avoid commitment to others. Others were running from the stress of a world gone mad. In most cases, they existed through those

days, never hurting anyone, never contributing to the better-
ment of the human condition, never preparing themselves for
a different life style.

And finally there were the seekers, the workers, the
achievers. Some of them were activists. Some of them used
drugs. But the excursions into self pleasure or social activism
were taken as sidelines, almost hobbies, meant to be brief
respites from their perceived "true purpose." They wanted to
make money, be a success, grasp the good life, and conquer the
world.

Sometimes the desire for success was a holdover from the
values of the 1950s when corporate life ruled the attitudes of
the young. Other times the drive came from fear—the war,
the Cuban missile crisis, the assassination of the president, all
served to remind them how fleeting success can be, how
transitory the good life. There was no time to build slowly;
they had to work hard to make it *now*. And anything that
would help them achieve that end was desirable.

One method was to use the potential of the human mind as
a way to influence others. A few years earlier, sociologist and
researcher Vance Packard had revealed the "hidden per-
suaders." He told about subliminal messages that influence
the subconscious, altering or reinforcing behavior. The public
learned that drive-in movies might flash messages so quickly
that the conscious mind would miss them, with only the
subconscious registering an unexpected desire for popcorn and
soft drinks. Advertisers used hidden sexual innuendos in
words and pictures so that their products would be equated
with sexual pleasure. Supermarkets had "canned music" with
hidden words saying "Do not shoplift. Shoplifting is a crime. I
will feel guilty when I shoplift," or they would have messages
suggesting the purchase of an expensive cut of meat or some
other item.

During this same period, the long-playing record was
becoming a staple in the average home. Albums were extremely popular. High fidelity and stereo equipment became

inexpensive enough that teenagers were spending millions of dollars on music. Musicians who could increase loyalty to themselves could get rich on record sales alone. Groups became desperate to find a gimmick that would make a difference in their income, and record company marketing personnel were working alongside them to see what could be done. Everyone stood to win, a fact that led some of them to begin exploring the world of subliminal messages.

Much of the information concerning what happened in the record industry comes from sources who must remain confidential. Engineers frequently insisted upon speaking off the record. Corporate executives were willing to be interviewed so long as their names and their companies were not identified. Even John Kappas, Ph.D.—one of the leading researchers in interpersonal relationships and the mind, an expert in hypnosis, and a pioneer researcher—though willing to talk, would not name everyone involved. Yet he knows what has been tried, what works, and what does not, and is still consulted at his office in Van Nuys, California.

"I first got involved in the early 60s. What happened was that I was getting an awful lot of musicians coming in [to my therapy practice] and people became very, very interested in the concept of how records affected people," said Dr. Kappas.

"These were guys who were in bands. Some were pretty big names, musicians, starting to come up. Others were just general run studio musicians, some record company executives. And I dealt with an awful lot of people in the record industry at that time."

Although Dr. Kappas would not discuss many of the clients, among those companies involved at the time were Capitol Records and groups such as the Beatles. These clients were *not* satanic, nor were they interested in Satanism. They were engineers, A&R people (artists and repertoire), promotion personnel, and rising groups, all of whom were concerned with finding ways to sell more records.

BACKMASKING

"They talked about, could we influence people by masking something and having it read backwards or subliminally so it could barely be heard on the tape. I said at that time that the subconscious mind is capable of all this, but I don't know to what effect. Let me test it out," said Kappas, recalling that period more than twenty years ago.

The desires of these groups, both publicly and privately, were not to corrupt the youth of America. They were not trying to place a "hex" on someone or otherwise do something devious. Instead they were simply interested in selling more records by creating as much of a following as possible. If subliminal messages would help sell, then they would use them.

Oddly, during this same period, Dr. Kappas was privy to the pillow talk of a woman whom he described as the "queen of the groupies." She was an extremely intelligent yet disturbed young woman who took pride in sleeping with all the major rock stars of the day, and she heard them discuss their plans for promoting themselves. "A lot of the input I was getting from her as to what some of their plans . . . what they were trying to do . . . most of it was to sell people on the idea of getting involved in sort of a momentum of buying records."

Dr. Kappas did not originate subliminal messages on records. Some musicians had already tried it, but they had no idea how successful their efforts had been without any serious scientific studies to determine whether or not such actions increased sales.

It was also found that the messages were not always commercial ones. Some of the musicians thought it would be funny to have hidden messages that would be considered antisocial. One musician recorded "dope is good" on the back of the music. Another used "join the club," and yet another stated his name over and over again. The main concern, however, among the majority of the musicians was to sell records.

The physical approach to backmasking is a simple one. A monophonic record of the day, played through a single speaker, might be considered a one-track tape recording. Stereo might be called two track because you hear music split between two speakers. The stereophonic quality begins to simulate a concert hall because each ear is catching sound from a different direction.

When professional recording engineers produce a master tape recording from which a record is made, they actually have many more tracks of sound—eight, sixteen, or even twenty-four. Instruments and vocals are recorded on different sections of the tape and blended together. You cannot discern the number of tracks when you listen to the music, but the extra tracks add to the quality of the sound. The sound can also be distorted from the original, making certain instruments louder or softer than they were when the group was playing.

As one engineer explained, suppose you have a twenty-four-track tape for producing the master record. From this the records for the stores will be made. A control panel allows the engineer to separately record, or not record, each of those tracks.

Now suppose you want to place a hidden message on the record so that it could only be heard when played backwards. You have twenty-four tracks, and you decide that track two will carry the message. The engineer then records tracks one and three through twenty-four normally, leaving track two completely blank. Then the tape is reversed so that the original tracks are now backwards. What had been track one is now track twenty-four. The blank track two is now track twenty-three.

Once the tape is reversed, the engineer throws the controls so that tracks one through twenty-two and track twenty-four will have nothing more recorded on them. These are the tracks with the music and the vocals. Only track twenty-three (formerly track two) is available for recording, and it is on this track that the backmasked message is recorded.

Next the tape is reversed once more. Twenty-three tracks will have music and vocals. One track will have a message that can only be heard if the record is played backwards. However, the musician who requested this work or the corporate executive of the record company involved with the addition, is counting on the subconscious mind registering the backwards words. These people believed that the mind would then correct the message and be influenced by it, resulting in more record sales and more name recognition.

The technique for backmasking described here is actually the approach used for the last several years. When the work was first begun, they did not know how to mask properly. "They would use a method to slow down a word, make it very, very slow in the process of mixing," said Dr. Kappas. "They would have a regular song with a slow word, hoping the unconscious would pick it up.

"It would be a softer track (than the rest of the words and music) and be in the background, and you had to concentrate very hard just to pick up the sound and you had to really step it up (increase the volume) to pick up the word.

"So what I did was that I took a pile of songs that were hits. And I took a bunch of young people, thirteen and fourteen years of age to twenty-one years of age, and I would hook them up to what they called biofeedback—galvanic resistance at that time—to see if there were high excitations or high melancholy feelings in the hit songs. I found out that of all the songs that I picked that were hits, all had either high excitation or melancholy. Usually the words had a tremendous effect on people.

"We also found out that when we had words that were not understandable but the beat was very, very prominent, it would give people kind of a wild 'up.' It would get them moving, almost like a hypnotic state. So we found out that in one respect, words had a tremendous effect on people. They

146

would create melancholy excitation, and the other would create, without words but just a beat, very heavy, dominating the words, this hype state the people were in."

The results of this type of music were several, though not the dramatic impact on the subconscious minds that some expected. Dr. Kappas explained that a group that wanted to intensely alter the mood of the audience would mike the instruments in such a way that they would be much louder than the singers. The group would use an intense, driving beat, the lyrics lost to the music. This driving beat would create a hypnotic effect that resulted in an unconscious escapism that had a long-term, residual effect on the listeners.

"To this day I still work with people from those days. I have to remove music from their brain. They can't concentrate or think because they are hearing music."

Those individuals were obviously unusually sensitive to the beat and more suggestible. "With some people, the music, the beat, and what they saw around them became a suggested idea. They became hypnotized by that kind of music.

"After that happened, they couldn't concentrate on their work. They would hear a sound every time they tried to do something; reading or studying, this sound would come into their heads. They couldn't concentrate, and in turn, they would avoid things. They would avoid responsibilities; they would avoid work, and they would start smoking a lot of dope. They would try to cover it up, hoping that they could suppress this sound.

"A lot of them thought they were going crazy. And some thought it was the Devil; all kinds of crazy things."

The cure was quite simple. These were individuals who were somnambulate, essentially walking around in a hypnotic state. They had let themselves become unusually sensitive to the driving beat of the music they had enjoyed years earlier, sounds that did not leave them.

Dr. Kappas would utilize hypnosis; then he had them imagine that they had a volume control for the music. He would have them imagine taking control of the volume, which was set at ten, the maximum sound. Then they would turn it to nine, reducing the intensity of the music they had heard in their minds for years. Next they would turn it to eight, listening to the sound grow weaker.

The procedure would take several weeks, each session resulting in a reduction of the sound. They were in full control, able to turn the sound back up if they desired, but they all gradually turned it down until, in a maximum of nine weeks, they no longer heard the music.

After the cure, the people who had suffered in this way avoided listening to the music they once enjoyed. The driving beat had become too painful for them. They became anxious when such music was played in their presence.

With this knowledge, Dr. Kappas and his researchers attempted to duplicate the results they were describing. They worked with backmasking, having words in reverse that were meant to provide subliminal messages. They wanted to see what effects they would have and even went so far as to place subjects in a hypnotic state to increase their sensitivity to the hidden messages.

The hypnosis was used to make the unconscious mind even more vulnerable to the messages and to keep conscious knowledge from filtering the impressions received. If backmasking worked, then the approach used for the study would increase the sensitivity to such hidden messages.

Dr. Kappas explained that at the time of his experiments, several facts were known. One was that the mind carried everything in a sequential pattern. When you hear words, your mind puts them in the proper, grammatically correct order. It also takes a word and turns it around when it is heard backwards slowly. "There are certain illnesses where people are affected by having some words reversed when they are heard. Given adequate time, the mind will reverse the words so that we can again make sense of them."

As the backmasked materials were played to a wide variety

of people, some proven to be more susceptible than others, several details were noticed. For one, words heard as sounds, without distinction because they had been recorded backwards for subliminal use, were remembered as they were heard. "If a word sounded like *burrrr*, it would be remembered as *burrrr*, not twisted and changed."

The results of the studies were several. First, there were enough teenagers and other subjects who reacted oddly to the backmasking for Dr. Kappas and his researchers to conclude that probably 5 percent to 7 percent of the population would have a bad effect from the backmasked records. They would become aware of the words hidden in the backmasking, not as specific words but as sounds they often found irritating to hear. The remainder of the listeners showed no reaction at all.

The testing continued, Dr. Kappas and his pioneering group of researchers attempting to determine an aspect of the mind that was extremely important. How could there be influence? What would the influence do to the individual? What did it all mean?

The first concern was with the estimated 5 percent to 7 percent of the American population who were sensitive to the backmasking. It was learned that the hidden words did *not* affect them with their messages. The message could be "I am happy. I feel wonderful. The world seems to have a special glow in my presence." Or the message could be, "I am depressed. I feel terrible. The only way to gain any peace is through suicide." In both cases, *the reaction was the same.* Instead of responding to the message, the person simply responded to the abnormal sounds. The listener was sensitive to the fact that there was a discordant sound on the record, the reality of the backmasking. The listener was not aware of the words.

The end result was irritation and mild depression for those who were sensitive; then they would wonder why they were feeling this way. Finally they would come to the conclusion that it was the particular record that was the link. They would say, "When I listen to this song, I get depressed." And then they would avoid the music, not buying the albums or singles. In the extreme, they might even turn against the musical group. Instead of selling more records and influencing more teenagers, backmasking worked to the personal and economic detriment of those who chose to do it.

"You see, the things that aren't understood about all these satanic things is how they get the message across to these young people. What you are talking about is what is called waking suggestibility. These are highly suggestible states easily influencing the young. They are influenced by fear of some kind of retaliation, of pain that will follow the message that you give them. They are extremely susceptible to these religious cults. They become the true groupies [for the rock musicians]. They become hung up on messages."

But these reactions are not caused by backmasked messages. Those lead only to a rejection of the record or the inability to hear or be influenced by the sounds. And this leads to a second discovery that came from this research—what is said consciously and how it is said influences behavior, not hidden messages.

For example, suppose someone is severely depressed, possibly thinking of escaping from their problems through suicide. "If a person wanted to kill somebody, I could make a tape that would affect the severely depressed mind, creating a situation that would result in that death. It doesn't have to be subliminal, and I don't have to say anything that would be an obvious danger to the public.

"What I would do is make a tape on which I took away all their future options. I would talk about the destruction of the world, the destruction of this country, atomic destruction, the fact that people are going to die anyway, and that our kids will never live to see thirty. Highly suggestible people would immediately become depressed and attempt to kill themselves.

"That kind of song would actually be acceptable. It would

150

fit the times. Like right now, people are on this anti-atomic power stuff."

Kappas explained that the use of options and the power of persuasion is common in many areas of life. Politicians attempt to do it all the time by trying to narrow our range of choices so that we vote for one particular candidate. In therapy, such changing of options is used positively, helping the person become healthier.

"There is a concept called the Message Unit Concept. Anxiety and hypnosis are synonymous because they use the Message Unit Concept to create the same effect.

"A record does the same thing. A record creates a message, an overabundant message into the brain. And if you get too many messages into the brain, you get a primitive mechanism that prepares us for fight or flight. If we can fight, we fight and we go into anxiety. And from the anxiety, which turns into almost an anger, it takes us into the depression. So just by that we can create the futile feeling that kids receive by overabundance of too many messages into the brain.

"That is why dope (marijuana, cocaine, crack, etc.) is so conducive during rock concerts . . . that what dope does is increase suggestibility of the people using it so that it makes them even worse." In addition, the availability of the dope at such a time makes the user want more in an effort to calm down. The user does not realize that the dope is producing the increased emotional response, so he or she may overload in an effort to reverse the emotional high.

All of Kappas's studies proved that people are truly susceptible to conscious messages on a record and that excitation and melancholy can be created by overload.

"We found that we could predict a hit record by first testing it on excitation and melancholy with the listeners. Then any conscious message that goes along with that record will be bought by the listener at that time. There is no defense against the conscious message received at that time.

"Any time you overload the mind, the person becomes very

suggestible. They will take in anything that you suggest at that time because they have no defenses against it. People can walk out of concerts in a hyper-suggestible state."

The result of this research meant a change in the attitudes of the major record companies. They stopped trying to provide subconscious messages and changed to working on the conscious mind, a technique common with advertising agencies producing commercials.

"Advertising uses a lot of overload music. It is like a mental bank. If I say that I want to become a millionaire and I am writing it at the same time, the mind will reject what I am saying but accept what I am writing.

"The same is true with music. Music has a tendency to diffuse thinking and create moods. And in turn, the messages seep in."

Although the record companies stopped backmasking, individual recording artists did not. Many engineers were cooperative, adding whatever words the artists desired.

"There is one song writer, very wealthy, very eccentric, who makes his money writing songs for other writers," explained one engineer who asked to remain nameless. "It's not well known outside the record business, but there are some songwriters who either don't write or are terrible writers. This man has written their hit songs. He makes millions of dollars, but he's eccentric.

"He lives in a mansion he seldom leaves. It has high gates and attack dogs patrolling the grounds. He often insists that his money be brought to him at his home, and because he makes so much, everyone cooperates.

"He had us backmask the records that have his songs on them. What we'd do is flip the tape and record whatever he'd want. Usually he'd have us add, '[name of major star] didn't write [name of song]; I wrote it.' He'd include his name and in that way try to have some recognition. It was both funny and sad. We'd always do it for him, and I don't think any of the

152

record companies or the recording artists ever knew what was going on. If they did, they didn't care."

The quality of the backmasking varied. One of the most controversial records was *Stairway to Heaven* recorded by Led Zeppelin. Words such as "I love Satan" and "Satan, Satan, Satan" supposedly exist on the back of the recording. It was a factor in hearings related to the record industry labeling practices held in Sacramento, California. Yet a tape recording of the record played backwards requires both great concentration and imagination. The word "Satan" does seem to be audible several times, but the way the sounds slur, any message is either lost or created more in the mind of the listener than in the reality of the sound.

"I question the reality of some of the records that are supposed to have been backmasked," said one engineer. "The track recorded backwards should be heard just like a normal tape recording when the tape is played backwards. In reality, the message is a normal recording, just one that has been reversed."

Surprisingly, engineers are reporting that when groups ask to have music backmasked, it is not just those who are known for their eccentricities or angry religious attitudes. Many are allegedly backmasked by Christian groups, though their message is usually something such as "I love Jesus." The engineers did not name specific records or artists, yet there is no reason to doubt the reality. According to Dr. Kappas, the positive message will be lost just as much as the negative one on the backmasked music.

"The only way to intensify the reaction to lyrics is to record them for conscious listening. However, they should be recorded slightly softer than the music so the person has to strain to listen to them. If you can add sensory deprivation, such as when someone listens through earphones, those words will take on extra importance. That's why music heard on those Walkman-type tape players can have such a strong influence if recorded correctly."

THE MUSIC OF OUR LIVES

Dr. Kappas and more recent researchers have all concluded that the backmasking of records, although a reality, does not subliminally alter the thinking of teenagers. Yet the other reality is that some rock groups are attempting to either leave satanic messages on their records or otherwise invoke Satanism with their music. Sometimes this is blatant, such as with the group that played under the name Black Sabbath. Other times this is more implied, such as with the group Kiss.

In talking with some of the musicians involved, as well as individuals they have consulted—researchers, psychologists, and psychics—a pattern becomes clear. Like so many others who have chosen Satanism over Christianity, they have a desire for immediate gratification and self-fulfillment.

"Money. Control. Power. They want the fantasy of being able to live a special life with a lot of wealth," said one psychologist whose practice includes some of the major names in the rock music business. "And they're willing to die young to pay it off. They see that by giving up life early, they can have everything.

"In other words, give me the first thirty years and you [Satan] can have the rest. These people can actually self-destruct. An entertainer can put himself in a mindset where he is preplaying his own destiny. And if he believes it strong enough, the guy is actually going to kill himself somehow or another."

The reality of this statement is obvious when you read the obituaries of rock stars. Many have died from alcoholism, drug abuse, or accidents resulting from their being under the influence of such products. The interviews with many of the stars indicate a live-for-today attitude that also infects many of their followers.

It must be noted that this attitude exists in another area of society as well—world-class, amateur athletics. In studies conducted by Dr. Irving Dardik, formerly head of sports medicine for the Olympics and an international consultant, many athletes actively seek drugs to enhance performance. Although it is now known that the use of steroids by athletes may lead to death through rare forms of cancer and other problems, the use of such drugs continues to be encouraged by coaches, parents, and peers. Dardik reported that many an athlete told him that "if they could take a drug that would guarantee them an Olympic gold medal but kill them five years later, they would take the drug without question. Their values put winning ahead of life, and it is not an uncommon problem. Some doctors are encouraging research into blood doping for bicyclists, hoping to find a way both to fool testing agencies and increase performance. We're talking doctors encouraging this. That's how bad this thing has become."

The obsession for power, fame, and achievement through a magic pill of one sort or another appears to be a major factor. With athletes, including those active in religion, the pill might be steroids or blood doping or something similar. With some rock musicians, the "pill" has been Satanism.

Does this mean that there are no problems with rock and roll? Not at all, but it is important to take the issue in context.

It is doubtful that any form of music is particularly harmful except, perhaps, when it is played too loud. Much of classical music was once the delight of a rebellious generation whose parents thought their children were going to hell with the raucous noise. The "Star Spangled Banner" is sung to the music of a bar song. Even some religious music has disreputable origins.

The language within some songs obviously should give parents pause, though that is a separate issue. The musical beat of rock and roll is also used by devout Christian musicians. One form conveys constructive messages while the other may not, yet if you remove the lyrics and just listen to the music, you might be hard-pressed to decide which type it is.

The fact that many children listen to rock and roll because

it seems like "their" music and engenders a form of rebellion is also nothing new. The ancient Greek writer Plato was one of the first individuals to decry the rebellious nature of youth, their laziness, and their disrespect for their elders. The "flappers" supposedly destroyed society, as did the "bobby soxers" and numerous other groups.

Most teenagers will listen to rock music and not join a satanic group or any form of cult. Most will reject the outrageous behavior of punk rockers, though the acceptance of these radical groups doesn't mean one has embraced Satanism. Many will use rock music as a way of coming to enjoy music and then explore the fields of classical music, Christian music, country, big band, and others. And their period of rebellion will be replaced by a conservatism against which their children will rebel.

Typical are the angry leaders of the sixties who wanted to smash society, drop out of the mainstream, enjoy drugs and forms of music that went against the culture. Many now head their own businesses ranging from serious art galleries to major corporations. In New York, some of the leaders who announced that no one over thirty could be trusted are now networking in order to link business professionals and advance corporate America. Even more shocking, they are forty and over, ten or more years past what they once thought was their prime as decent human beings.

The hostility towards rock and roll has led to certain myths about the music. For example, many critics claim that rock and roll actually means a sex act. It is referring to a couple making love in bed. They attempt to find phallic symbolism in the music.

The truth is that rock and roll is nothing more than a style of heavily accented two-beat jazz whose origins trace back to what is sometimes known as "race" music. Some gospel music has some of the same roots—a simple melody, often based on the blues, scored for small groups. Originally this meant rhythm and saxophone for many musicians when rock and roll evolved in 1954. The vocals and instrumentals had harsh, reedy tones, with lyrics that were primarily based on adolescent romance problems.

If you listen to rock music today, most of it imitates the past with simple and often adolescent lyrics about first loves, romances, or love entanglements.

Other records are designed to shock and have themes that border on the obscene. The rock star Prince sung about public masturbation, and taboo sexual words are frequently heard from some groups. But these are not in the majority.

Oddly, many people have forgotten the less obvious, yet equally immoral lyrics in songs by Gershwin, Cole Porter, and many others, and sung by entertainers such as Frank Sinatra. "If I'm not with the girl I love, I love the girl I'm with . . ." goes a line from one song. "Love for sale" was a popular blues line. "Ten cents a dance" covered the Taxi dancing, a highly disreputable way to make a living when the song was popular. And "Gigi," a movie that would be rated "G" today, was actually the story of a woman raised to be "kept," a monogamous prostitute as it were, although she triumphed by marrying the man who was originally designated as her "keeper."

Obviously these examples do not make the sexual innuendos found in some of the lyrics acceptable, but they do keep them in perspective. We are not seeing a radical change in society because of the music in general.

At the same time, if children or teenagers are obsessed with music, and music groups assume role model identities, then parents should be concerned.

In a very small number of people, a fraction of the five to seven percent of the population that researcher Dr. John Kappas has found is at all sensitive to what amounts to a noise layer caused by backmasking, satanic messages used in rock music (or Christian messages used in Christian rock) can have an influence. But not through backmasking. The message

157

comes from the lyrics that they are using, reinforced, at times, by the stage presentation.

With "tons of repetition," a message in favor of Satan spoken in the lyrics would start to be believed by the long-term listener. "They would start feeling a conflict between their morality [the way they were raised] and the new morality that is given to them. Chances are if they didn't get any relief from their morality by saying, 'no, that is not true' [to the message in the music], they would try the morality of Satan, if they got a relief from that. If they did, then they would follow that," explained Kappas.

Other psychologists agree with Kappas, stressing the timing of adolescent exposure to repetitious lyrics. If the heavy involvement with those few rock groups encouraging satanic messages occurs during a stage of rebellion, the effect can be severe. If a child is rebelling against parents, he or she would attempt to search out or create a counter life style. This may mean attempting to become involved with Satanism, reading about the field, listening exclusively to such music, and similar actions. It is an act of rebellion against the family unit.

"It would be a conscious rebellion that eventually would turn unconscious if you did it over enough consciously," explained Dr. Kappas.

To what end might that lead?

"Realistically that could lead to someone's self-destructing. That could lead someone to become sadistic, masochistic. . . . It could lead to antisocial behavior, psychopathic, to all kinds of sick things."

And how long might that take? Most therapists feel that the time depends upon how suggestible the child might be. Generally such children are either underachievers—more intelligent and with greater abilities than their grades indicate—or overachievers—working unusually hard and long to accomplish grades that would not be possible if they worked the same amount as their peers. They are either very positive or very negative, yet they are obsessed with life in either direction.

The result of all this is that a child can be drawn into satanic practices and thought processes through an obsession with the wrong type of musical lyrics. When those lyrics are presented in a manner that results in mental overload, such as rock music, the susceptibility increases. If the lyrics are innocuous, as so many of them are, then there is no problem. If the lyrics are Christian, the end result should be positive, although the means to that end—obsessive listening—is not. But if the lyrics are satanic by design, a child runs the same risks as though obsessed with the fantasy games that promote evil over good.

CHANGING OUR TUNE

Fortunately there are ways to spot the problem. The first answer obviously is to be aware of your children's music. Although not all albums have the lyrics printed on the back, those that do can be checked by parents. This is the ideal answer and many people feel the record companies should routinely do this. It would be legal under the First Amendment to the Constitution since free expression would be protected, and parents could simply say no to the purchase of records with offensive lyrics.

A second approach is to use a rating system much as is used in the movie industry, but critics say that this becomes a form of censorship. They also feel that it would be difficult or impossible to agree upon standards. Even with the film industry, controversy continues over the fact that a film with voluntary sex between consenting adults shown in a tasteful manner (the couple is married, the covers are over their bodies, and no flesh is shown) may receive an R rating while a martial arts movie with extreme violence may get a PG. Similar problems are likely to arise with lyrics.

The third approach, the banning of the records, perhaps coupled with mass burnings that have been practiced by a small number of clergymen, is the least popular. Critics feel that such actions lead to totalitarianism. Some fear religious extremism; others remember Hitler's burning of books that failed to match his beliefs. "Let the record companies producing such trash go out of business because no one is buying their products," said one mother of a teenager. "I fear the censors more than I fear any impact on my son from this garbage some of the groups are playing these days."

A parent can easily spot the changes in a child if the parent is willing to look. "What you recognize is that the child is walking around in what we call a minor anxiety state. In turn he is overmedicating himself [taking drugs and/or alcohol] possibly to bring down anxiety," said Dr. Kappas. Not all teenagers will take drugs, though all those obsessed in this manner will "show a lot of signs of depression and anxiety."

The depression and anxiety will be far greater than what might be considered normal for a teenager. "He will be having very strong difficulty in coping with anything. He is escaping. He would either try to isolate himself, becoming a loner, or he would try to be with a group all the time. The group would be similar to him. They would be down in the dumps and escaping."

There would also be other signs of this type of overload. Their eyes would not look normal. "They can't think straight. Their talk is a little like stuttering. They are affected by loud sounds, movements, motions, voices. There is no tolerance towards stress. They are completely down."

At this stage, the child often goes to concerts hoping to escape. He or she reacts to form, voices, people talking loudly. The stereo will be turned on loud, a fact that changes the escape to a greater problem, something the child does not realize.

"After a while, depression feeds depression so anxiety feeds anxiety. Loud music would feed the overload to keep them constantly overloaded. They are smoking [marijuana, crack, etc.] to bring down the overload and it increases their

160

suggestibility and, in turn, overloads them again. So they need more and more and more.

"Finally they develop bizarre behavior to compensate for that 'thing.' It is almost like the excessive-compulsive neurotic. He becomes excessive-compulsive to avoid some hidden voice process in his brain. He figures that if he works real fast, he is going to run from it. He really doesn't.

"We can spot them. During hypnotism we spot these people instantly. And I would say ten to fifteen percent of the people that come in for the first time this way are hyper-suggestible. We have to de-hypnotize them instead of hypnotize them. That is a high percentage."

And what should a parent do when a child is exhibiting all of these symptoms?

"The parent should immediately attempt to seek some professional help for the child. A parent actually can't really help the child. The child does need some professional help," said Dr. Kappas.

"Now let's assume if you were going to write a manual for parents on how to help these children, what we would do is tell them not to fight them. Don't create any more anxiety in them. Talk to them about being on their side, giving them a lot of options out of this feeling. It will be okay. We are for you. Give them a lot of reinforcement.

"The parent should subtly reduce the time the child is listening to the music. Don't do it a lot because it will cause an anxiety in reverse. Just slowly reduce the amount of music. Cut down the volume first and then the amount, and gradually try to get the kid into seeing a lot of different options, a lot of different activities, feeding them into the brain."

Interestingly, the problem described also exists for many adults in the record industry. "I have one company that had five or six of their key employees sent to me, and when I was finished with them, they began sending others," said Dr. Kappas. "They all come in for different reasons. They come in because their relationships are falling apart. They come in because they can't concentrate on their work. They come in because they are feeling depressed all the time. But the reality is that they are overloaded and have no tolerance for relationships.

"They are playing the music constantly. They are involved with the record business. They are listening to songs. They are getting the songs promoted. They constantly have their ear on the radio to see if their songs are being played. And it overloads them."

The problem is not with the music but with the lyrics. "What music does that has no words to it, it triggers mood. And in turn, your mood becomes a center of attention and you relax. Words keep you going."

What type of music is best for relaxing? According to Dr. Kappas, "It has to have sort of a monotone stage to it, not too many highs or lows. What that does, it leads your thoughts into moods and feelings, and that is what we use to develop creativity.

"That is how we teach someone to write music. We find something that puts them in the same kind of mood. If they want to write a depressing song, we find a song that depresses them. We have it playing in the background. There are no words. Just the music. And all of a sudden it opens up the right side of the brain and they start flowing."

DEVIL-MARKS

DEVIL-GIRL: JESSIE?

She called herself Jessie as she fled across the country. She was young, in her early twenties, attractive, the kind of girl parents would delight in having their sons date—at least until they saw the tattooed pentagram on her left arm.

TRAPPED LIKE AN ANIMAL

Jessie's story began in the Southwest. "I was sitting in a bar in Lubbock, Texas, and I had never been anywhere east of Lubbock in my life. These guys came in. They had funny accents—one of them was from England and one of them from Boston, and they talked me into having a mixed drink. The last thing I remember is handcuffs on my hands in the back seat of their car, and they took me away."

Jessie had been working for the Temple, Texas, Independent School District but moved to Lubbock after she had a fight with her boyfriend. After she took a job with the Carriage House Motor Inn, she and some of the others started going over to the bar after work. They would have a beer and share conversation, the bar being a friendly neighborhood location where everyone got to know everyone else. This was a habit she had followed for six weeks, long enough to be considered one of the regulars.

When the two men ordered her a drink, they were strangers, not likely to be remembered. They were able to slip a drug in Jessie's drink, though what they used is not known. All that is certain is that Jessie began to have trouble moving her legs. "I got confused and then I couldn't talk, and the next thing I knew, I was in the back of this car."

The next few days were a nightmare for Jessie. She was raped repeatedly, though by whom she never knew. She was always blindfolded and handcuffed during the rapes. They would also whip her, the whip digging deeply into her back, a fact that has left scars to this day. ("Her back looks like hardened raw hamburger," according to one police officer who saw her.)

There was a third torture as well, the one that proved most effective. The men would force her head under a water faucet, squeezing her nostrils shut while her wrists were handcuffed behind her back. Her mouth would be forced open as she fought for breath, but instead of air, water would fill her lungs. No matter how much she fought the water, eventually it would enter her throat and lungs. Sometimes she would choke violently as they let her up. Other times they would let the water flow in until she lost consciousness, then use artificial respiration to ensure she would continue breathing. A slight error in their calculations and Jessie would die, a fact of limited concern to them.

The two men who raped and tortured her kept stressing to her that they wanted her soul. She had to give them her soul to make them stop. Nothing else would matter.

Just what was racing through Jessie's mind during this time, she does not recall. It is doubtful that she ever experienced any sort of internal theological dialogue relating to the meaning of

God, the role of the sufferer, and the question of whether or not God could allow such pain to be experienced by an innocent victim. This was not a case where she thought about whether or not God had forsaken her. All she knew was that the pain was endless and that if she sold her soul to them, they might stop. She agreed.

There was no momentous change when Jessie sold her soul, no sounds of trumpets, shaking of the earth, or anything else—only the simple relief of being allowed to stay alive. What she did not realize was that her action would become a psychological wedge in convincing her that she was lost to Satan for eternity.

The two men stopped abusing Jessie. They placed her in their car and drove her to New York City where they met with the lead singer of a well-known rock group. He purchased Jessie to be his "house pet."

The role of the rock singer in Satanism is unprovable at this writing. After Jessie's eventual escape from white slavery, efforts were made to place her in contact with the FBI. However, the offices contacted expressed no interest. No one was willing to take her statement. No one felt that she was a priority, though she had described a white slavery ring that violated both local and federal laws in at least two states.

What is known for a fact is that the rock singer was an acquaintance of Anton LaVey, and Jessie was told that the singer followed "LaVey Satanism." Her impression was that LaVey at least knew of what was going on and that he may have been involved. Yet without documentation, this cannot be proven. The friendship between LaVey and the rock group leader may have been as innocent as the friendship between the singer and the other members of his band.

Jessie was told by the singer that three people effectively ran the Church of Satan in the United States, the singer being one of them. Yet that may have been a statement made by a braggart, not one that is factual. Tragically, because of jurisdictional disputes, no legal action has been taken in

167

regards to Jessie's circumstances, though some individuals Jessie knew have been arrested in routine vice cases.

Jessie's life was dominated by fear and bondage. She was neither loved nor trusted, only used.

At first the routine involved conditioning her to the singer's control. When he was home, and he maintained places in both Boston and New York City, she was allowed complete freedom under his supervision. She could not leave without him, but she could clean, cook, and otherwise take care of his home.

Some of the singer's friends knew that he had a "groupie" living with him. They were told that it was alright to have sex with her, and they took advantage of the situation. Jessie had not been a virgin when she was kidnapped, but the sex she enjoyed was within her control, an aspect of the commitment she had made to her boyfriend. She would have been hysterical had anyone suggested that she would be available to any man who wanted her, yet by the time her kidnappers had broken her, she accepted anything that happened. Survival demanded such acceptance.

When there were strangers present, reporters doing interviews, or other individuals who might ask questions, Jessie was locked in the basement. She was the singer's secret as well as his property.

Nights were the hardest for Jessie. When she was ready to go to sleep, she would be handcuffed and then tied to the bed. At first the bondage made sleeping difficult, and her wrists and arms would cramp. Then, gradually, she adjusted until, when she eventually escaped, she found that she could not go to sleep with her wrists freed. She had to take a scarf, tie it into a loop, and slip it over her wrists in order to restrict movement. Only then could she rest.

Jessie was desperate to escape, yet she was afraid of the singer. Her arm was branded, actually tattooed with the sign of the pentagram in a circle. She learned that she was not the only woman who had been victimized in this way, though the

168

others were now prostitutes working the New York to Boston corridor. They had been emotionally broken, then tattooed and placed into white slavery, and forced to act as prostitutes. Some truckers have indicated that the branded girls were well known, and though some had purchased their favors, the truckers were nervous around them. They feared the person, unknown to them, who ran the organization that they recognized as being satanic.

The girls referred to themselves as bitches, a loosely used term for those whose role it was to have sex. Jessie was a house bitch, though she discovered she was not alone. A male within the music group was similarly kept for those times when the singer wanted a homosexual relationship. It would eventually be the male, who felt his own escape was hopeless, who would help Jessie flee captivity. Together, when cleaning the house or preparing the meals, they would sneak enough beer to get drunk and help each other emotionally to whatever degree they could.

Eventually Jessie made her first escape, returning to Texas where she had friends and family. According to Rusty Carroll, the Assistant District Attorney in Belton, Texas, Jessie met two brothers who lured her into the woods, allegedly related to some sort of drug deal. So far as the investigators have been able to determine, the action involved a satanic ritual.

One brother grabbed Jessie and slashed her throat with his knife. She played dead, even as the other brother grabbed her head, jerked it up, and held a Bic lighter to her face. He said, "Yeah, brother, you did a good job. Now you're one of us," according to Carroll.

"There was other satanic involvement—ritual books and satanic tattoos, much stuff along those lines. I had to try that case twice. The first time it was reversed on appeal and we had to try it again.

"She's who she says she is. She runs away from that guy in Boston with great regularity. She's legitimate."

As horrible as Jessie's life had been, she had a tendency to return to the man who kept her prisoner. One reason was her parents. According to one sheriff's deputy, when her parents came to visit her in the hospital, they informed her they wanted nothing to do with her. She was considered an embarrassment to the family, a disgrace. The people whom she needed most of all were also the ones who turned away from her when she was in the greatest need.

Another reason was the brainwashing the singer had used on Jessie. She was convinced that after she gave up her soul to Satan, God wanted nothing more to do with her. She believed that if she even stepped into a church, she would be killed.

During a period when she was visiting with Ted Schwarz, one of the authors of this book, and his wife, she was asked to come to their church. She had expressed an interest in architecture and their church is a large, old stone building that is listed on the Historic Register. She admired it from the outside; yet when it was suggested that she go inside, she became hysterical though there were no services at the time and the minister was not present. To enter a church meant death in her mind. God would strike her down for entering his house, and then she would live in hell for eternity. No amount of reasoning would calm her. The fear was too intense for rational thought.

A third factor was described by Carroll. He saw her as fitting the classic abused wife pattern because of the emotional abuse by her parents. Such emotional abuse and rejection by those she most desperately wanted to love her could easily have caused her to accept the singer's violence. She may have felt that she deserved nothing more.

THEIR HANDS TIED

Jessie's story raises a number of serious questions when exploring contemporary Satanism. The most important is the issue of what is satanic. Is Jessie possessed by the devil because she sold her soul after being tortured and raped? Or is

Jessie a helpless victim whose action has no meaning other than keeping her a prisoner in a sadomasochistic lifestyle?

And what of the problem she has with churches? She has been told by her kidnappers that she is ruined for life, permanently estranged from God, her eternal fate completely sealed. She is not likely to voluntarily work with any religious program because of the way she has been abused.

With law enforcement, the problem is even greater. The law can't prevent the voluntary return of a victim to someone who has been her kidnapper, her jailer. Jessie accepted the life style of the rock singer who "owned" her even as she desperately tried to flee. She feared prosecuting him because of the power his money could buy. She was terrified of being away from him, knowing he was hunting her, convinced that the punishment for being away would be greater than the horrors she would face if she returned. She chose a known fate, no matter how horrible, rather than the unknown fate of regaining control of her own life.

Law enforcement officers responded differently in different areas to Jessie. A number of local police units were willing to help her make her way across the country. They believed her story, had faith in her honesty, were comfortable with her escape. Some law enforcement officers filed reports, but the problems of improper jurisdiction or legal limits always thwarted due process. In some instances, she feared to prosecute because of the wealth and power of the men involved. In other instances, such as the Texas case, the prosecution only involved one level.

Individuals with the San Francisco Police Department, Dr. Lois Lee, founder of Children of the Night (a Los Angeles-based organization that helps teenagers in forced prostitution), and others attempted to get the FBI to interview Jessie, all to no avail. Eventually the Los Angeles County Sheriff's Office did record Jessie's story for the official files, though Los Angeles County did not have proper jurisdiction over the crime.

Oddly, a man claiming to be a private detective, working with the FBI in the San Francisco area, called one of the authors of this book. He said that some investigation into Satanism was being conducted quietly by the Bureau. He was either volunteering or being paid to run down leads on this problem, perhaps doing some preliminary interviews, then passing the information on to his contacts within the FBI.

The man was a private investigator, and his general credibility was confirmed. Yet when I talked with law enforcement officers about talking with him concerning cases they had shared with me, their general attitude was that they would only speak with the FBI directly. They, too, felt that cooperation with the government had been limited and did not wish to talk directly with anyone other than an FBI agent. This could not be arranged, and it didn't seem safe for Jessie to be interviewed by a private citizen.

The reasons for the refusal by several different Bureau offices are unknown. According to a check with the U.S. Attorney's office, white slavery and forced prostitution when existing between state lines are crimes covered by Sections 2421 and 2422 of the United States Criminal Code.

One comment, made by a vice squad detective, was that a jury would probably not be sympathetic to a woman who may have been a prostitute, and she would be presumed guilty, not to mention how involvement in Satanism and rock music might prejudice the jury. The case would sound too ridiculous and off the wall to be real.

As the detective said, "The fact is that whores are not our favorite people. If someone came to me with the story, I'd talk to her. But I'd be thinking of her as some slut rock groupie who's probably carrying every kind of disease known to God and man. Should they have? Sure. Why didn't they? Maybe they were tired. Maybe they didn't want a hassle with someone who sounded like a nut. I do a better job with some people than others just because of the way they come across to me. It's hard to say, but I can see it happening."

Another reaction came from an Assistant U.S. Attorney. "It's a judgment call. How did the woman call in? What was said? Did she say, 'I know of this going on, and a lot of girls are being hurt,' and when they asked her for details, she said, 'Well, I can't really supply any, but I know it's happening.'

"Or did she gives names, dates, specifics they could investigate?

"Did the FBI know of a state or city law enforcement agency that was investigating the same thing and had done more than they could do? It is a crime that falls under federal jurisdiction, but with any particular incident, it would be a judgment call."

The harsh reality of this type of circumstance is that both the victims and the average citizen are forced into the position of being investigators in order to be certain of attention. Yet without talking with the woman, without seeing the tattoo and scars, and without hearing the information from Texas, it would be difficult to believe her story.

Another problem comes from the fact that the motivation for the crimes is unusual. Was Satan masterminding a kidnapping ring? Or did a group of men choose to make money in an illegal, demeaning, often violent manner, justifying their actions through their involvement with Satanism? Either way, if the satanic involvement was mentioned in a court of law, would that statement make people think less of the case? Would mentioning Satanism cause the jury to take the case less seriously?

One prosecutor, speaking off the record, discussed his attitude towards Jessie and cases like hers. This is a man who has been involved with child molestation cases with satanic overtones and other controversial prosecutions.

> I wouldn't want to be involved with this one. First you've got the character of the girl. She's young and she wasn't a virgin when she was kidnapped. A lot of people would see her as kind of wild and loose. The

173

fact that her parents don't want anything to do with her might work against her, too. Maybe the parents are bad people. Maybe you see some residual adolescent rebellion problems coming out. Maybe she has a history of being involved in things that aren't too nice. You can bet the defense is going to know these things and use them against her to hurt her credibility.

Then you've got the fact that she wasn't always held captive. There were times when she was with the group in public. There were probably times during the shows when she was there but unguarded. You know and I know that if somebody's terrified and abused, they'll act like a hurt puppy. They'll wait for you to kick them again because they're more afraid of what will happen to them if they leave. But you try telling that to a jury that has never seen it before. They're going to believe that no matter what happened, she wanted it.

Now you got some celebrities in this thing. They're people who don't need a slave to get a little sex. They've got groupies just waiting to jump in the sack with them. They've got money from their records, money from their concerts. Why would they want to get into something like this? Again, if I was the defense attorney, I'd bring in a bunch of CPAs [Certified Public Accountants] to show how many millions of dollars the celebrities earn from their business, how many millions of dollars they earn from their investments, how much in taxes they pay a year. Then I'd get some of the prostitutes on the stand to talk about how much they get paid for turning a trick. What do they charge today? $50? $100? Whatever it is, it's going to look like nothing compared with their other income. And I don't care if the guy has one thousand girls working for him. A thousand girls you can't imagine. But one girl, on the stand, under oath, talking about a $100 trick after you've just heard respectable CPAs talking about millions is not going to be very persuasive.

By the time the case was presented, your Jessie would be in the right. The pictures of her back where she was beaten would be dramatic. That tattoo you described on her arm would have its impact. But I think she'd come off as a vindictive slut wanting revenge against a lover who threw her over for a prettier woman. And I don't think I'd get a conviction. . . . They'd be trying Jessie and finding her wanting. Like I said, I'm glad I'm not directly involved with this one.

The third problem is one that arises with any criminal case. Justice is frequently determined by which side has the most money, the greatest access to the media. This is not to say that justice can be "bought." Rather it is a matter of having the resources to bring a case into court. It costs money to find all possible witnesses. It is expensive to hire expert testimony from men and women who may have to be flown from throughout the United States or even from a foreign country. Funds are available for the minimum defense of those without money, but the minimum defense may not be adequate.

In the case of Jessie, if she were to stand alone against the rock star who kept her enslaved, she would need several types of experts. These would range from law enforcement officers to individuals who are expert on the "battered wife" syndrome, the psychological damage from the forced prostitution, and similar matters. A local psychologist might not have the expertise, plus a recognizable name might sway the jury more. Certainly the rock star, a man worth millions, will use whatever resources he has to keep himself from jail. His side will have these types of experts. Her side will need them.

Is Jessie's case unusual? Yes and no. It is unusual in its allegations against men of such notoriety. It is also unusual in that there appears to be a nationwide network, although a small one, involved in the crimes, if her statements are true.

Yet a check with law enforcement officers throughout the United States indicates that her story fits small scale vice operations they have seen. Individuals are running prostitution who claim to be satanic, and some will have tattoos, perhaps possess *The Satanic Bible*, and talk about various rituals. They may subject the women who work for them to unusual sexual practices based on their religious beliefs.

Yet many satanic pimps may be using Satanism as a justification for antisocial behavior. Whether this is a backlash against the way they were raised, a joke to scare the women who work for them, or the result of some other motivation, is not known. All that is certain is that women such as Jessie are in the minority, a fact that makes her suffering no less real, her problems no easier to manage.

DEVIL-CHILDREN:
UNTOLD ABUSE!

I was 12 years old. It was the summer between 6th and 7th grade . . . This took place over a period of 3 nites and 2 days . . . Kept inside the house the whole time . . . Mostly locked in Hannah & Jane's room . . . Sometimes Dad's room . . .

During early evening of all 3 nights put in shower naked . . . hands tied around shower head with rope lengthened a little so were allowed some movement . . . Dave and women each took turn showering me tied up there . . . Sometimes they'd alternate turning hot & cold water on me for a while . . . During that time they had the lights out so it was very dark . . . During 1st night after I'd been in shower most of the evening . . . they untied me . . . Elaine wrapped me in a towel fixed my hair . . . taken to living room naked . . . no light on just candles . . . this procedure was repeated all 3 nights. . .

Aside from such writings by twelve-year-olds, the story of Anton LaVey probably serving a leg of lamb and convincing people maybe, just maybe, they were practicing cannibalism seems a harmless practical joke. The thought that it might be possible to say a few incantations or perform a ritual that will cause some special man or woman to fall passionately in love seems attractive.

Maybe Satanism isn't so bad. Perhaps its only crime is that the practitioners are a little naughty, a little immature. Some of the leaders in the better known groups seem like eccentric showmen, but the followers couldn't really be hurting anyone because the police would catch them. The stories of murder and torture in the name of Satan couldn't really be taking place.

And then you heard the stories about the children again and again.

My friend's daughter told her mother what happened to my son. The little girl is almost 11 and my boy is 8. She said that the two teachers took him out to the barn in back of the day care center. It's in a converted farm house, almost all of the land around it having been sold off.

She said she saw one of the women take a rope that was hanging from the rafters. She tied my son's hands, then pulled on it so he was suspended a little ways off the ground by his hands . . .

My friend's little girl said she couldn't take her eyes off my son's face. He was crying and crying, but one of the teachers told him not to cry.

My boy was scared of pencils when he came home from school. He said they hurt you.

He was talking about oral sex. He was talking about abuse. I took him to the doctor and the doctor said there were marks in his rectum consistent with what he had described, but there was no serious injury. He said it could even have been done by my boy experimenting with putting things in various openings of his body. He said sometimes kids do things like that. He said he didn't believe my boy did it, but he would have to admit to the possibility if he was called to testify in court.

We arrested a woman who worked for a preschool day care center. She was taking the children and subtly molesting them. She would take one child and tell the child she was her favorite. She would give the child special treats, have her sit on her lap, comb her hair, or whatever gave the child pleasure.

She would only do it away from the others so the children never knew it was happening to several in the class. Then she'd begin touching them sexually, giving them good feelings. She never told them not to tell anyone. She never threatened she would do harm to them if they talked. She never told them it was a secret.

She was good. If she had threatened them, we probably would have learned about it sooner. Some child would have been afraid to go to school. Some child might have talked. But the parents had all told the children how good teachers are. The children were taught to trust the teachers at school and so they were not afraid. She made everything seem natural to them.

When we finally learned what was happening, we asked her why she had done it. She said that she was a Satanist, that she had decided that she would win Satan's love by corrupting an entire generation of children. I don't know how many kids she had molested, but she had worked there for four years.

I also don't know how many complaints we'll have for the court. One psychologist said that the way she abused the children was the most subtle you could use. The kids saw nothing wrong. She was gentle, loving, giving them positive feedback. He said that it's only when the kids reach puberty that we might see some results. He said that usually in these cases of positive molestation, either the child realizes what happens, feels tremendous guilt for allowing it, and decides that he or she encouraged it, or the child cannot have a

179

normal sexual life. The adult becomes hung up on kinky sex or some deviation. Either way you're looking at a need for therapy that may never be expressed. If the child was terrified, it actually is easier to get him help.

We're going to send her to jail, but we're not going to be able to use her statements. If we go straight child molesting, we've got a case. We've already got some of the kids talking and I think we'll have no problems. But if we add the Satanic pact she talked about, the jurors will probably laugh us out of the courtroom.

Child molestation and murder are the two areas where even the most accepting individual becomes wary of people declaring themselves Satanists. The messages received from people such as Anton LaVey are mixed. The writings imply that some actions should not be taken unless they are absolutely necessary. And to a deviant mind, what is necessary can be extreme. Even more frightening, there are times when like-minded individuals with the same abnormal desires and behavior join together in groups. The molestation becomes ritualistic, and the large number of people involved adds an extra intimidation factor for the child.

I didn't know what was happening until my four-year-old daughter had a nightmare one night. It was the most terrifying thing I had ever witnessed. She was writhing on her bed and saying, "Don't do that to me. It's nasty." It amazed me that, at her age, she knew the word nasty. But that's what she said. Not, "It's not nice," but "it's nasty."

Then it was like watching a pornographic movie. She threw her arms back. Then she stripped. She literally took off her pajamas and underwear. She put her hands above her head like she was tied up. . . . And that's when the eyes opened and she started screaming. "Please don't hurt me. Please don't do that."

And then she would turn over . . . and scream that it was hurting her. And this went on for about ten minutes and then she would stand up in bed, and then she collapsed. And then she went deep asleep.

I couldn't react. I just stared at her, trying to understand what was going on. And then the next morning I knew I had to question what was happening.

Children make the best victims because they are the least credible and most easily fooled. For example, in one police case there was definite proof of child molestation but the allegations went much further—children being forced to drink blood that had been taken from their bodies. One boy said that the blood was taken from the back of his leg, and that story was repeated by others. Yet the pediatricians examining the children said that there were no veins that could be used in that manner in the areas the children described. They also said that there were no marks indicating any needles had been used.

In other instances, the children talked of Superman, cowboys, or some other figures being involved with the abuse. One parent mentioned that his son had described a well-known movie actor and karate expert as being involved. However, upon further questioning, the child did not say that the man had been present. Instead the group had shown him a picture of the star, whom the boy knew from movies, and said that the actor was one of their leaders and would hurt him with karate if he ever told what was happening.

Children have described not only murders but also the burial of bodies, usually those of small babies, in a particular section of a yard, field, or park area. The descriptions are so vivid that law enforcement officers have obtained the necessary warrants to dig for evidence. In some cases, the ground appears to have not been tilled in weeks or months; in others, there is some evidence of digging. Yet in all the cases, neither bodies nor bones nor pieces of clothing have ever been found.

181

They had this infant. It was really tiny, like it was just born sort of. And they gave me this dagger. It had some sort of design on it. And they had me hold it and one of the people in the cult put his hands around mine so I had to hold it. Then he told me to stab the baby and he forced my hands down again and again.... This happened when I was 12.

LOVING CHILDREN TO DEATH

In one west coast case, the district attorney's office had three teenaged girls testifying against a group of men who they said were involved with satanic activity. The men allegedly molested the girls, including forcing them to endure "cleansing rituals" such as scalding showers or hot candle wax on their genitals. They were also made to participate in the making of "snuff" movies in which babies were killed.

The girls all had scarring in their vaginal area that was consistent with what would be expected if they were forced to endure the physical abuse they described. The marks were also consistent with damage that, in theory, no human would voluntarily self-inflict. The pain would be too intense.

The problem came with the snuff movies. A snuff movie is a film in which someone is killed, usually as a part of a sex act. The first came to widespread law enforcement attention more than twenty years ago when it was rumored that films were being made for lovers of sadomasochism. There would be violence as part of foreplay; then the woman would be killed during the sex act. Sometimes this was a simple strangulation. Other times she was tortured first and then raped while dying. But always there were the allegations that the actress was actually murdered.

Such reports about snuff movies were enough for intense investigation by everyone from area law enforcement agencies to U. S. Customs. The Mexican Mafia may have been either the conduit for the transportation of the films or the manufacturer. An effort was made to identify the actresses who were shown murdered, and in some instances, the women were identified. Yet with only one proven exception, the early investigations found that the deaths were faked. The actresses lived to play other roles in other pornographic films.

The three teenagers testified about the babies being used. Their statements seemed credible because of their ages and the marks on their bodies. However, such films did not and have not emerged. No evidence has been found to support the charges that the group was practicing ritual murder as part of their satanic ceremonies.

The market for child pornography films is unusual at best. According to one customs official, pornography films have not changed much in the last fifteen years. Others familiar with the industry claim that there is little or no commercial production of child pornography films of any type. Instead, it is a cottage industry fueled by the low cost of videotape equipment.

"What we're seeing is Daddy taking the kids into the garage for an afternoon of fun and games," said one cynical investigator. "The bastard shoots this garbage, usually using his wife and their friends, then trades it to people he knows. The tape never goes to a processing lab where it might be caught by an inspector. It can be duplicated with a cheap machine and hand delivered to people who want it. This guy could have made a thousand tapes, but so long as none of the kids talk, we're never going to see the product."

Some child pornography networks have been identified. Frequently the groups will use computer modems and the telephone lines to keep in touch. The employees of one real estate agency are under investigation for allegedly using vacant houses from their listings for child pornography films.

Child pornographers do not necessarily have an interest in snuff movies or Satanism. Some are pedophiles, that is, those who prefer children as their sexual objects. Others are disturbed in different ways, delighting in some type of violence or abuse. Only a small minority are involved in

Satanic worship and many of these tap into the pornography underground to obtain children for rituals.

"Alice took the bucket, the one she used for cranberries. There was blood in it . . . she poured the bucket of blood on my hair and then I was dead."

"How did you know you were dead?"

"I don't know. I just was."

"How did you come back alive?"

"My mama took me home and combed the blood out of my hair and then I wasn't dead anymore."

UNHEARD CRIES OF CHILDREN

A child's world is not that of an adult. The ability to reason, to interpret experience, and to understand what is happening in the way that an adult understands, is extremely limited.

Dr. Martin Reiser, the police psychologist for the Los Angeles Police Department, discussed one of the problems with child witnesses, especially children under the age of five. He told of one case where a four-year-old was able to vividly describe a murder that had taken place in the next apartment. She said that she had seen the murder through the window, and the investigating officers were delighted. They thought they might be able to make a case against a suspect as they listened to her story.

Although the child's story seemed to be verified by what was found at the crime scene, some of her facts did not make sense. The officers asked the child to show them where she had been standing in her mother's bedroom. The child took them into a room, pointed to the television set, and said, "I was watching that window there." She did not know the difference between the television set and a window. What she had observed, by chance, was a television movie about a woman murdered in almost identical fashion.

Some investigators feel that the only times children are believable come when either there is corroborative physical evidence or the child describes something beyond logical chance. For example, if a child describes a choking sensation and the man's ejaculation, it is probably true. The younger the child, the less the chance that it would be possible to make up such a story. Certainly it would not match anything the child could fantasize from life experience.

Yet when a child talks about being dead, then being alive, when a child says certain abuse occurred, but there are no marks on his or her body, these statements must be questioned. Even worse are the cases where part of the information is credible and part of it cannot be believed.

I can't speak on the record about all this because we have no proof. One of the problems we've been facing in law enforcement is locating the corpses of the kids we think have been killed. We're told highly credible stories by children who have either helped with a murder or witnessed a killing; then there is no body.

What I think is happening is this. In some instances, we've identified molesters with some connection with funeral homes. We had one guy who ran a funeral home and another one who worked for one. We even had a security guard once who stayed in the place at night. The owner trusted him completely and showed him how equipment such as the crematorium worked. The owner was certain it had not been used when the security guard was on duty alone, but he also admitted there would be no way to tell for certain the way the place was set up. We think that either some of these kids are being buried like the old Chicago funerals where the coffins had a mob victim on the bottom and a legitimate corpse on top, or that the bodies are being burned.

The other suspicion we've got is that they're buying babies one way or another. We had one crazy in here who was pregnant and told us she was giving up her baby as soon as it was born. She claimed she was part of a cult group and she was pregnant so they

185

could sacrifice the child. I don't know if it was true or not, but if they delivered the baby themselves, there'd be no record of the birth. And if the woman was a stranger, no one would question what happened.

They might also be buying them down in South America somewhere and bringing them up here. But that seems a little far fetched. I think it's more likely some of these groups really do have members who will have babies just for the rituals. It would be the simplest way to go and no one would ever find out.

Publicity about missing children has led some law enforcement officials to investigate the idea that a number of them may have been kidnapped for ritual ceremonies. This is a possibility, though there are a number of problems with this idea.

The vast majority of missing children are runaways or kidnap victims. Of the kidnap victims, many are taken by a parent when that parent has been denied legal custody. Such children are usually safe, well, and loved.

However, some children are missing because they have been sold to someone. Computerized sex bulletin boards list children for sale and tour agencies will organize child sex vacations for pedophiles. In countries where poverty is rampant, the selling of children can be a means of financial survival. Some families have adopted foreign children specifically for sexual use. Such commerce in children has made it easy for Satanists to obtain them for rituals.

In order to have a pornographic picture of a child, an adult must commit a criminal act. Thus every picture taken, whether or not it is published, is the permanent record of a crime. Since the child lacks understanding of what is happening and has to be coerced, there is no such thing as consenting involvement.

Healthy adults should not find children sexually arousing. The people who read child pornography magazines are abnormal and their motives far from healthy. Their actions are condoning what, for most adults, is already the unthinkable. It is easy for them to be willing, if unwitting, partners with those Satanists who involve children in their ceremonies.

Teenagers involved with Satan worship seldom utilize children in their rituals. Their actions are more likely to involve either animals, other teens, or adults. For example, five teenagers ranging in age from sixteen to nineteen were arrested after the body of a nineteen-year-old was found in a cemetery in Pennsylvania. The five alleged murderers claimed to be Devil worshipers who had nothing against their victim but just wanted to watch someone die. According to the autopsy, the victim had a pipe placed behind his neck; then a bandana was put around his throat to choke him. He was beaten unconscious about the head and face with the pipe. A cigarette lighter was used to set his hair in flames.

Prior to the arrest for murder, one of the youths stole a car by slashing the neck and arm of the driver. Again the violence was more from curiosity than anything else.

In another instance, a teenager who worked as a stripper in a nightclub was horrified to see her parents in the audience. The girl had become involved in a satanic cult, began using drugs, and was engaged in casual sex for hire. However, much of her life was hidden from her family, and she was outraged when a friend revealed to her parents just what she was doing. Her reaction was to convince some members of her cult that the proper action to take was to murder the youth who talked.

Investigating officers found that the girl and her friends regularly held Satan worship services. They prayed to Lucifer and tortured dogs, cats, and other small animals as part of their rituals.

Not only have teenagers not been shown to involve younger children, but also their motives seem different from the adults. The teens are often troubled, rebellious youths with difficulty relating to school, parents, and life in general. Some become immersed in heavy metal music, which may have themes that support their feelings of alienation, anger, and revenge. Others become obsessed with fantasy games. Some turn to Satanism to shock, to belong, or to justify personal actions that go against the way they were raised.

The truly troubled may sacrifice household pets, or neighbors' animals; and some, after this experience is acceptable, may kill humans, though rarely children. Perhaps it is harder for a teenager to find a way to obtain a child. Perhaps it is because, in any city, teenagers are familiar with young drifters who will not be missed, so they focus on the same people chosen by many religious cult recruiters, pimps, and others who prey on the young. Kidnapping and murdering a teenager or young adult satisfies the demands of Satanism and is relatively easy.

Whatever the case, adults seem to kill children, teens kill each other, and the police are in the middle of it all. One east coast detective commented:

> We have no trouble catching the kids. They are young, naive, talk too much, leave evidence behind, and otherwise reveal themselves.
>
> A few are so into Devil worship and drugs that they think they are invincible. They practically walk up to you, hand you the weapon, and tell you to arrest them, then are surprised when you actually link them with the crimes they've committed.
>
> The real problem is the adults. They know how to cover their tracks better. They'll convince the kids who are molested that they saw things they didn't see. They'll trick them. They'll get them to say things that any adult knows can't be true so when they tell what really went on, nobody believes them. And if you do prove that a crime was committed the way they say, then take them into court, there's a question of what will happen if the questioning becomes too thorough. They start talking about people dying, then getting up again, burial sites that don't exist, or anything else . . . their credibility is shot.

The other problem is that these people are able to get rid of the evidence. Sometimes by the time the kids are talking and anyone believes them, two or three years have passed. Other times they have used fairly sophisticated methods for destroying the bodies or burying them.

The reality is that if you want to use a human in one of these things, a child is the best one to use. They're not credible witnesses to many people, and they're also the best victims.

There is one other aspect to ritual child abuse. Frequently, when the child is either molested or used in a violent ceremony as something other than the victim, the action is made to seem pleasurable. The child becomes the leader, the special one, the person to whom the other children must look for guidance in the group.

"They gave my son special robes," said the mother of a boy who was both molested and helped molest others in a day-care center.

The adults treated him like a little god. They gave him special privileges and they never threatened him. Anything he wanted was given to him and he delighted in it. I didn't realize how serious this was until he began giving orders to his younger brothers and sisters and they would obey him. He told them horrible things, things even the most curious of little children won't do. And they did them. They seemed absolutely terrified of him. It was like watching a dog that has been beaten so many times that it whimpers and cowers when anyone approaches.

And my boy was only 7. I can't let him live at home with the other kids. My mother's caring for him and I tell you, I'm afraid of him. I've got him in therapy, but I don't know how long that will last or what good it will do. I keep wondering what he's going to be like when he gets older, when he can be a danger to adults. It's terrible to say that you're afraid of your own child, but I am.

Children are afraid of retaliation. They have been told that their parents, their brothers and sisters, and their pets will be killed if they talk. They are often shown animal mutilations as a scare tactic.

An Arizona psychologist who has handled a number of satanic-related child molesting cases from day-care centers sees a complex problem:

> The tragedy is that the people doing the molesting in day care centers and similar locations have an advantage. The vast majority of them are good, honest, decent people. Parents rightfully tell their children to trust the teachers, to do whatever the teacher tells them. If the teacher says the child has been disobedient, the parent will rightfully take the teacher's side.
>
> So you get a situation where the teacher is bad and the child has no say. He knows the parents will side with the teacher. He knows the teacher is hurting him, terrifying him, but what can he do. And if he finally gets the courage to tell the parent, and if the parent believes the child and removes him from the situation, weeks or months may have passed. The child has been the victim of the damned and not even the parents could save him. The long-term damage this might do we're not sure we've even begun to understand.

Not all Satanists are child molesters and many Satanists find the idea of using children for any type of ritual to be reprehensible. At the same time, child molestation cases with Satanic ritual overtones are a serious and growing problem for law-enforcement agencies.

Normal molestation cases involve certain consistent patterns, such as pedophilia, an emotional sickness where the adult genuinely loves a child and cannot comprehend the taboo against sex with that child. The Satan worshiper who engages in such acts deviates from the predictable. He or she may be viewed as the pillar of the community—a doctor, lawyer, school teacher, or even a member of the clergy. There is no psychological disturbance as currently defined in the standard training literature. There is no anger against the child, no abnormal love for the child. The child is a means to an end, a part of a ritual for which the Satanist may have no more feeling than he or she would for a hammer and nails, the tools used for building a house.

The result of this situation is that it is difficult to successfully prosecute the molester. Juries tend to want a motive that is easy to understand. Ritual abuse is not only hard to comprehend, it is rather frightening to consider. Instead of a monster being seen on the witness stand, the person charged with such a crime may be well dressed, attractive, and have dozens of character witnesses willing to testify on his or her behalf. As a result, many cases are not taken to trial and many others are lost.

Even worse is the fact that each loss in court emboldens the Satanist. The person feels protected, knowing that he or she is guilty, yet also certain that it is only because of the Satanic blessings received that the triumph occurred. Each act reinforces the next, endangering an ever-greater number of children.

What is the answer? It is hard to know. Many law-enforcement agencies are hoping that educational programs for the general public will help put the issue in perspective. Others, fearing witch hunts, hope to find enough evidence so that the motivation, and thus the issue of Satanic worship, does not have to be brought into court. But whatever occurs, it is the children who are suffering because of the adults' difficulty with coming to grips with this nightmarish problem.

DEVIL-DODGING: FINAL THOUGHTS

Talking or writing about contemporary Satanism is always a problem. When we started this book, we were constantly criticized for our early findings. Fundamentalist Christian groups were against our saying that certain circumstances were not as bad as they claimed. For example, the satanic influence in the music world has not proven to be any more a reality than the satanic influence in law, medicine, banking, or anywhere else. The fact that musicians are entertainers and thus are paid to flaunt what at times is outrageous behavior makes them more visible. Yet far more doctors, lawyers, and clergy are convicted of child molestation in cases where law enforcement officials have claimed, off the record, that there was strong evidence of Satan worship, than anyone in the music business.

Law enforcement officers have been nervous about our discussing the satanic involvement in many child molestation cases. They admit that it is a factor, often the driving force for the offenders. Yet they also know that such cases are hard enough to prosecute at best. When the full extent of Satan worship is known by a jury, they become uncomfortable and sometimes acquit the defendants rather than accept the involvement.

Mainstream church leaders have sometimes criticized our

work because they feel it may glorify Satanism. They fear that someone reading about it may wish to try it. They are concerned with the popularization of the religion.

And the Satanists have frequently been irate. They are concerned about whether the information will be presented objectively. Other times they have subtly threatened by saying, "Satan will not allow you to succeed." And the hidden message is that the speaker is an emissary of Satan, thus the conveyor of the threat and the potential source of the punishment.

The research for this book has taken almost five years. Extensive files have been created with hundreds of contacts developed among law-enforcement officers, religious groups, Satan worshipers, psychologists, and others. Interviews have been conducted with people ranging from Satanists to their victims. We have put together what may be the most accurate and objective overview of the subject within recent years. So what are our conclusions?

THE EXTENT OF THE PROBLEM

First, another church really is down your block. The number of people practicing Satan worship in any form, whether organized or by a few individuals, is fairly small. Yet these people are probably in every community in the United States. Larger cities are likely to have covens and other organized groups. Surprisingly, some small towns are the same way, though many will have only a few Satanists often operating without knowledge of one another.

Some of the Satan worshipers are serious members of a group such as the Church of Satan or the Temple of Set. Some form their own groups, frequently using *The Satanic Bible* as their guide. Some are loners; others attempt to be serious scholars of Satanism; and a few use their version of Devil worship to justify perverted and/or illegal acts.

Some Satanists are obvious deviates, strung out on drugs and looking like the type of people you want to meet in a dark alley only if you are carrying a cross and a high-powered gun. But most are ordinary individuals, perhaps your friends or neighbors. They may be doctors, lawyers, school teachers, bus drivers, laborers, or almost anyone else. Frequently, they look as though they would be perfect to head the PTA, the bowling league, the country club social committee. Even more upsetting is the fact that sometimes they do. The average Satanist cannot be recognized except through his or her actions. Unlike Christians who usually worship publicly, Satanists conduct their rituals in private; consequently, it is very difficult to identify who is a Satanist.

IS SATANISM GROWING?

This question is difficult to answer. If we were to compare known Satan worship today with what took place in the early 1960s, the answer is probably that it is. Yet these things are cyclical as has been shown, and today the media is more sophisticated in transmitting information throughout the country. There is more awareness and a greater willingness to talk about the problem. In addition, we are in the same cycle of insecurity that affected the nation in the 1950s, the last big period for occult interest.

The growing interest in Satanism may have been caused by the continued alienation many are sensing from the traditional church. Christ's message has been lost in religious jargon and viewpoints.

Some Christian leaders are seriously studying the Bible and their opinions are borne out of scholarly research but also much prayer. They are humble enough to admit that they don't have all the answers and are tolerant of anyone who is truly worshiping the Lord.

Others either have perverted the Word of Christ or are presenting questionable concepts. Some of these have *the* answer, condemning anyone who may question their word to eternal damnation. Others preach that god power is green power. If their followers are not rich, they have done evil because God's people are not poor. This is preached despite the fact that Christ and many of his followers were poor.

Some have created political groups such as the Moral Majority. In the meantime, some people question how religion and politics should be separated, becoming angry with what they see to be a perversion of the church's leadership.

And there are those religious leaders who seem to be greedy, albeit for God's work. Most television evangelists have more calls for financing than they have calls to the altar. Jesus was never recorded as taking up a collection following the Sermon on the Mount. In fact, he was the selfless giver of food for both the body and the soul. Some simply report strange occurrences. The historical works of Flavius Josephus, the only known contemporary historian to record information about Jesus' existence, does not reveal anything unusual about Christ. Neither did the disciples see him as anything other than an ordinary man in physical size. This means that he was probably around 5'4" tall, normal height for his time, and he managed to change the world for the last 2,000 years.

Besides the antics of the traditional church, there are the shenanigans of the religious cults. Although scholars give many definitions of cults, one generally accepted has certain key facets. First, the leader is usually the stated or implied Christ in his or her second coming. Second, knowledge is carefully limited and often filtered through a group of elders in the group. Third, the members are constrained in what they can think through positive measures. They are "love bombed" when they join; their talents, real or imaginary, are praised. They are immediately involved with any number of projects, often taking up eighteen to twenty hours a day, thus depriving them of sleep. New members' diets are often restricted to further limit their ability to think about what they are experiencing.

The satanic groups seldom follow the cult logic. Even Michael Aquino's implication that he is the direct connection with Set on earth does not hold for his followers the same significance as a cult leader claiming his second coming glory to his disciples. Thus it is easy for Satanists to attack the cults and, indirectly, Christianity, because Satanism is so different.

Both the occult and many cults welcome life's losers who are desperately seeking acceptance. Yet the occult goes a step further and condones those actions that might be taboo for Christian cults. These can include greed, adultery, torture, and murder. Such freedom of choice for the emotionally healthy may be okay; but for the disturbed mind, this creates options that may lead to disaster.

When Christianity rejects troubled people, they sometimes turn not only to cults but also to Satanism.

In some instances, the church may reject its own by not following through on its beliefs. For example, it is one thing to oppose abortion; it is another to provide the long-term emotional support needed by pregnant teens.

Likewise, look at the number of entertainment figures, political leaders, and other "names" who have come to God. While average people are often given excellent support—brought to Bible studies, helped through crises, and given years to develop—a celebrity is treated differently. Too often famous people are asked to give testimonials, be role models, and instantly be perfect Christians. When the celebrity backslides, no one reaches out to help and support that person. Instead, the pious ones say, "The Devil's got him again. We'll have to stay away from him because he's with Satan, not the Lord. Such a tragedy . . ."

And when there is hypocrisy in the church, the weak condemn all of Christianity instead of seeking a God-loving group. Some eventually drift off into the occult, letting Satanists fill their lives with meaning.

Satanism on its own might not be on the rise, but the church by its practices is giving it many willing victims.

HAS SATAN TAKEN CONTROL OF OUR AIRWAVES?

Jim Bakker's confession of adultery and Tammy Bakker's admission of prescription drug addiction began a radical change in television evangelism. The Bakkers, who headed the PTL (Praise The Lord or People That Love) Club and the Heritage USA theme park, became the most discussed television evangelists in recent history. The press focused on these television evangelists who had been making hundreds of millions of dollars from their followers. While the press delighted in showing the mansions, the million-dollar earnings, and the many perks, the faithful attempted to understand what was happening.

The simplest answer for many of the followers was that the devil had taken control of the evangelists' lives. Satan was in Jim and Tammy—or Jimmy, Jerry, or Oral—depending upon the viewer's attitude towards the specific minister. Such good people had waged an ongoing battle with the Devil, and the Devil had proven too powerful. The best get taken first, the Devil flaunting their fall to show his power on earth.

Many people put their faith in Jimmy Swaggart, who denounced Bakker as a cancer on the face of Christ. Then they discovered that he too was being accused of committing sexual acts against the teachings of the church and this also proved shattering.

One woman, a former university student of one of the authors, contacted him with the question of whether or not she was sinful for having been led to Jesus through the ministry of Jimmy Swaggart. She was having difficulty separating the man from his religious statements and separating both from Jesus. Was she sinning because her heart had been changed by Swaggart's message about the Lord? If he had failed, was she likewise destined to fail? And could she still love him for the positive influence she felt he had had in her life even though he had fallen in her eyes?

There were many issues raised, including the concept of the

Lord often choosing the most unlikely vessel for His work. The former student talked with the author about Moses, who had difficulty speaking, being used over his brother, who was articulate. The biblical prophets were discussed, none of whom found favor in his time.

Equally tragic was the circumstance where people were shocked to learn that Jimmy Swaggart would not respect a suspension by the national Assemblies of God, primarily because it would cost his ministries too much money. He obviously needed help to rid himself of what he discussed as an immoral sexual obsession. Yet seemingly the money had become more important than feeling right with God and the church. Did this mean that he was preaching the gospel of greed? Or did it mean that his personal life had to be separated from his words? Or could he have simply become devil possessed. Was this really Satan's revenge for his stepping into the fight against the "possessed" Bakkers?

Yet the simplest answer may be giving Satan too much credit and be saying more about the public's own self-deception. The more success someone has, the more we want that person to be in tune with the Lord. Likewise, the more controlled our view of a given person, the more we idolize them and make of them what we will, regardless of what they are.

The more people watch television, the more they create fantasy lives. Vanna White of "Wheel of Fortune" is a perfect example of a fantasy creation. Vanna turns letters, but she hardly ever speaks. Her education, interests, and abilities are never discussed. She is a high-priced, flesh-and-blood mannequin. So far as anyone knows, she may be an intellectual giant who could solve international problems. Or Vanna White might be a bimbo, a body without a mind who has to work hard just to turn letters. Whatever the truth between these extremes, the adoration of Vanna White has become enormous.

Men find Vanna White the perfect wife, daughter, and lover.

Girls want to emulate Vanna. One publisher paid her a six-figure sum to produce an autobiography regardless of the quality or need. Her television image has become reality for thousands—each one certain that *their* Vanna is the real one.

The Vanna White phenomenon carries over into our attitude toward television evangelists. If a man or woman looks good on the screen, sounds caring, talks of love, and gives us hope for tomorrow, then we look upon the person as almost saintlike. Yet the reality is that we know nothing other than that the person is a good entertainer. We are manipulated by what may be a carefully crafted image.

The reality is often quite different from the image. It is known that many television evangelists live extravagantly. They live in mansions, drive luxury cars, own expensive clothing, and delight in the hedonistic experience of great wealth. Unfortunately, the extravagances are likely to continue. A television ministry can be a vehicle to bring the Word of God to more people than would be possible otherwise; but at the same time, it can be a way to assume pride, glory, and an unusually high income. Even when a salary is relatively low, royalties from books, movies, records, videotapes, and similar sources often will add a million dollars or more to the gross receipts.

We seldom really know television evangelists. If they make appearances in different parts of the world, if they show photographs of poverty, of missionaries, of proposed structures, we feel that they are doing good works. If they say that God has spoken to them and ordered them to achieve certain ends, we assume that they would neither lie to us nor deceive themselves about their calling. We feel uncomfortable asking for an accounting of donated money. We believe in what they say because we want to believe in them.

We overlook their lack of one-on-one counseling. Some do have special programs for follow-up, but others will play the numbers game, quoting the sizes of their audiences as though each of those is a soul permanently changed and dedicated to God.

Often they perform miraculous healings that are of a questionable nature. In some instances, elderly but extremely healthy individuals have been placed in wheelchairs. When they are called forward, they stand up and walk, something they have always been able to do. Yet to people watching their television sets, the image is of a cripple miraculously being healed. This fraud may be enhanced by claims from the minister as he praises the Lord and the camera freezes the shot. Meanwhile the audience at home thinks that the person was always confined to a wheelchair.

In essence, we deny the possible realities of television evangelists. We assume that they are saints and never consider the possibility that they may be extremely weak in their personal lives at best, and dishonest at worst, when they enter the ministry.

By making these assumptions, we create our own illusions. Believing these frauds to be honorable, we are shocked when they are caught and we assume some recent change has occurred. The fact that a longtime crook or con artist has just been shown to be what he was all along is often not considered. We just can't accept the fact that we might have been misled. Although Satan is at work in this world, we may be rationalizing when we blame a minister's fall on the Devil. We are afraid to smash our idols and admit they have feet of clay.

The fact that we can be brought to God through dishonest and disreputable individuals speaks well for the Lord. He can use an unlikely vessel to show his hand in our lives. But it is what we then do with our new understanding of Jesus that matters, and the actions of our human mentors should not turn us from following him. Because the image of God has been defaced but not erased in humanity, bad people can do good works, but good people can also act despicably.

All of which brings back the question of whether the fall of media celebrities ranging historically from Aimee Semple McPherson to Jim and Tammy Bakker means that Satan is triumphing in radio and television land.

If Satan is involved, we are to blame for giving him too much power. All Christians are aware that when the name of Christ is invoked, evil has no power. The adversary is rendered impotent by the act. The ongoing struggle with Satan comes from our desires, our pride, our corruption, and we can stop the internal warfare in a moment by changing our hearts. Bad people have and will speak in the name of the Lord, often with great success. Good people will fall and rise again through God's grace. Satan has not gained power over the television evangelists. Those who fall once and change are like everyone else trying to find his or her way with Jesus. Those who fall repeatedly, regardless of their claims to the contrary, probably have yet to reach out to Christ.

WHAT ARE THE GREATEST THREATS FROM SATANISM?

For the young, the threats of molestation, psychological damage, and even murder are more common inside these extremist groups than law-enforcement officers want to admit publicly. So long as jurors shy away from convicting people with alleged satanic connections, such atrocities will continue. Thus we must be realistically on guard when helping our children through the early years of life. We must warn against not only stranger danger but also the familiar person peril. The family pediatrician, the beloved teacher, or the trusted neighbor may be the culprit.

For the teenager, the danger comes from negative obsessions. A truly obsessed teen is frequently disturbed, whether the fixation is Satan or Christ. Endless hours of playing Dungeons & Dragons and of listening to radical counterculture music can be harmful. Even the Bible and Christian music can become a negative obsession if they are used to escape reality rather than face it.

201

Parents need to become familiar with their children's favorite music. They should not be put off by the unusual clothing or hair styles of the entertainers. Every generation rebels against the previous, though most adults will not admit they may have defied their own parents. We should listen to the lyrics of songs and attend the concerts to see what is taking place. Then we should place appropriate restrictions, not on lifestyle but on inappropriate and unhealthy actions. We can focus on the worst and ignore the rest or develop an uneasy truce. Otherwise the rebellion can be more extreme.

When obsessions do take place, professional counseling may be in order. Fantasy games, music, and other areas may become abnormal fixations. Sometimes fantasy games lead to an interest in the occult. And in some cities, drug dealers have discovered that occult fanciers are easy prey for their chemical expanders, so drug addiction becomes an additional problem for troubled teens and another trauma for parents.

We must realize that children and teenagers are influenced by more than just the home environment; the media, peer pressure, and numerous other factors affect them. Neither parents nor children should consider counseling a stigma, and clergy, school counselors, or professional therapists can be very helpful.

Sometimes counseling reveals the differences in perceptions between children and their parents. Children reveal the inability to communicate with parents, and their parents express guilt and inadequacies.

The past with all its mistakes should not be the parents' focus. A child's well-being is more important than a parent's pride. It is critical to seek help early rather than wait for a child to outgrow a problem. Too many children are obsessed with fantasy games, Satan worship, and the music of alienation, with the result that depression and sometimes suicide follow. The results have been too well documented for parents to turn their back on them.

For adults, it is important to recognize that Satan worship is real, that it is more than theater or people acting a little strange. Nice people are involved with ritual molestation. Nice people are committing murder in the name of Satan. Their numbers are few, but they are in every community.

We can get involved in positive ways. We can visit our children's daycare centers periodically rather than just dumping the children there on the way to work. When local law enforcement makes an arrest for a crime with ritual overtones, we should at least be willing to consider satanic involvement. The Devil is not "going to get us" because we are willing to speak up against those who are abusing others in the name of Satan. Such worship is not an epidemic corrupting America, but it is taking place. Accepting the reality is the first step towards stopping the practitioners from hurting others.

Again, it is important to remember what Officer Sandy Gallant of the San Francisco Police Intelligence Unit tries to stress. If these people are real, if they are truly tapping into the power of Satan, then Christ is always stronger. The good of the Lord will always dominate over Satan. And if they are not tapping into such power, then they are hurting other people for their own depraved reasons. Whatever the case, they still must be stopped.

ARE PEOPLE POSSESSED BY THE DEVIL?

This is a tricky question. The answer that many people want to hear is that such possession is impossible, that it is the fantasy of the supposedly enlightened religious person. Others want us to say that, of course, possession is possible, that it is the root cause for all sin. And still others want to be able to use the name of Satan to justify every excess in which they indulge ("The devil made me buy this new dress or expensive car, commit adultery, or gamble at the racetrack").

From a historical perspective, we have to rely upon the Bible for guidance. The New Testament has Jesus casting out demons, though there is little mention of Satan himself entering man with the exception of Judas Iscariot ("Then

Satan entered Judas, called Iscariot, one of the Twelve"—Luke 22:3). Yet the very fact of the statement concerning Judas, if taken literally, means that Satan can, indeed, enter a human.

Assuming the reality of Satan, as most Christians do, it would seem that possession would be possible. However, in the cases that have been explored, and these involve literally hundreds throughout the United States, no sudden, born-again-in-hell experience seems to have occurred, though the individuals involved were open to the idea of possession and were seeking satanic powers. As often hurt and alienated people, they were anxious to experience the dark side of life.

For example, in Santa Cruz, California, a child-abuse victim eventually became involved with murder and other forms of violence. The person claimed to be a Satanist, and some respected religious leaders felt the person was possessed; yet when his teen years were examined, it was found that the person, at seventeen, had actively been playing with the Ouija Board. He told friends that he wanted to enter the spirit world and have all the power of evil because God had forsaken him. He opened himself up to the worst in the universe because of anger and self-hate; and if he were possessed by Satan, he had invited him into his life.

In Phoenix, Arizona, a boy went to jail after pulling a series of robberies. The psychologist who examined him was also a minister and felt that the boy was possessed.

Once again a check of the history shows that the youth wanted to be satanic. He had started with obsessive playing of Dungeons & Dragons, delighting in both evil and consistent winning of the game. Then he determined that the dark side offered power he could not achieve through his family's Christianity. He began spending time at occult bookstores. He read about rituals, developed his own ceremonies, and eventually sold his soul to Satan. Then he began robbing banks, convinced that he would not be caught. To his surprise, he ended up in jail.

In Florida, Texas, Pennsylvania, and every other state that

has been studied, the pattern is the same. If both young people and adults have been possessed, they have actively sought it. Whether or not their actions are simply the result of purposeful wrong or directly the evidence of satanic possession, is a matter for argument.

Tragically, some of the individuals interviewed felt that they were trapped. In one instance a Texan talked with a Lutheran minister in Arizona about ritual abuse, murder, drugs, and violence that he had seen in a Satanist Church. But he also bragged about the money he had made and the women whose sexual favors he had enjoyed.

The man left Satanism and worked as a short-order cook in Flagstaff, Arizona, but he was not happy. He missed the casual sex, the respect of others, and the money. Neither did he not want to love the Lord nor reach out to others. But he cared about physical pleasure more than love and commitment.

In the end he quit his job and moved to Las Vegas, Nevada, where he knew some practicing Satanists. There he found women, money, and drugs. He deliberately turned his back on all that we might consider good to lead a self-centered, potentially destructive existence in the name of Satan.

Possessed? I doubt it. A Satanist? Without question.

The problem with most studies of satanic possession is the lack of information. What have been the Satanists' problems? What have been their choices? What actions have they constantly taken that led to the situation where they might be viewed as "possessed"?

The television and the motion picture industry have also distorted the idea of possession. The fantasies of *The Exorcist*, the *Omen* trilogy, and related films often are viewed as realities. If someone says that a film is based on a true story, the average viewer assumes that it is an accurate reflection of a genuine circumstance.

The authors of this book have been involved with both television and the motion picture industry. One of the authors had an earlier book shown on television as a docu-drama that was based on a true-life story; yet if anyone read the book, which was one-hundred-percent factual, and compared it with the movie, the only connection would be the character names. The story was fictionalized for the most part in order to provide dramatic impact.

It is only when you look at the reality, not the fictional representation, that you truly know what occurs. And, to date, no cases investigated indicate any individual was spontaneously taken over by Satan. Equally important, when the person reaches out for help to Christ, whether directly or with the assistance for an intermediary, he or she is made well again. Satan may have power, but we are the ones who have the control through Christ.

WHAT CAN I DO TO FIGHT THE PROBLEM OF SATANISM?

Beyond the suggestions already made, we must truly understand the problems faced by those who end up in Satanism. We can work with youth to alleviate pressures and build their self esteem.

We can be open and loving to other adults by not condemning those who fall, not giving up on the troubled, or not shunning those who are different because of race, religion, or anything else. Our lives will speak more of Christ than our worship, our friends, or our money. We will be judged by others for our actions, and our influence can do more to keep someone from going down the path to Satanism than we might imagine.

Satanism, like drugs, has a strong appeal—instant gratification of desires, a chance to do that which would otherwise be taboo, and an opportunity to give ourselves to total personal pleasure without fears, anxiety, and regrets. Likewise a person has no growth, commitment, or long-term happiness.

Satanists often need the same support as those who have been on drugs—reinforcement for positive actions and acceptance after failures.

Some practitioners of Satanism seem silly in their beliefs and actions while others appear to be monstrous in what they do. All of them are serious and not to be dismissed lightly. This is a problem that exists in every community, though on a much smaller scale than many believe. Through awareness, prayer, loving interaction, and supporting law enforcement agencies, the most reprehensible of the problem areas can be reduced or eliminated in the years ahead.